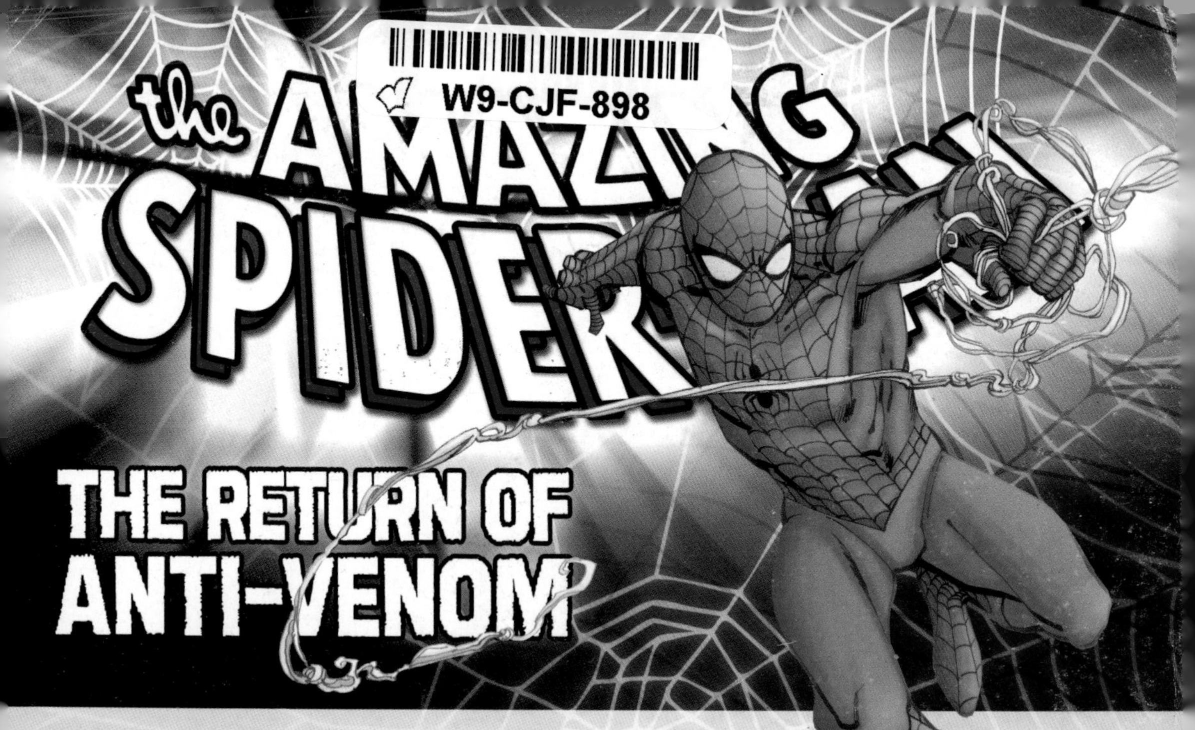

REE COMIC BOOK DAY 2011
Vriter: **DAN SLOTT** • Penciler: **HUMBERTO RAMOS**
nkers: **CARLOS CUEVAS** & **VICTOR OLAZABA**
Colorist: **EDGAR DELGADO** • Cover Art: **HUMBERTO RAMOS** & **EDGAR DELGADO**

SSUES #663-664
Vriter: **DAN SLOTT** with **CHRISTOS GAGE** (#664) • Penciler: **GIUSEPPE CAMUNCOLI**
nker: **KLAUS JANSON** • Colorist: **MATT HOLLINGSWORTH**
Cover Art: **FRANK CHO** & **PAUL MOUNTS**

SSUE #665
Vriter: **DAN SLOTT** • Penciler: **RYAN STEGMAN** • Inker: **MICHAEL BABINSKI**
Colorist: **JOHN RAUCH** • Cover Art: **PAOLO RIVERA**

"THANKS...BUT NO THANKS"
Vriter: **TODD DEZAGO**
Artist: **TODD NAUCK**
Colorist: **CHRIS SOTOMAYOR**

"I'LL NEVER LET YOU GO"
Writer: **DAN SLOTT**
Artist: **GIUSEPPE CAMUNCOLI**
Colorist: **MARTE GRACIA**

Letterer: **VC'S JOE CARAMAGNA** • Assistant Editor: **ELLIE PYLE** • Senior Editor: **STEPHEN WACKER**

Collection Editor: **JENNIFER GRÜNWALD** • Editorial Assistants: **JAMES EMMETT** & **JOE HOCHSTEIN**
Assistant Editors: **ALEX STARBUCK** & **NELSON RIBEIRO** • Editor, Special Projects: **MARK D. BEAZLEY**
Senior Editor, Special Projects: **JEFF YOUNGQUIST** • Senior Vice President of Sales: **DAVID GABRIEL**
SVP of Brand Planning & Communications: **MICHAEL PASCIULLO**

Editor in Chief: **AXEL ALONSO** • Chief Creative Officer: **JOE QUESADA** • Publisher: **DAN BUCKLEY** • Executive Producer: **ALAN FINE**

PIDER-MAN: THE RETURN OF ANTI-VENOM. Contains material originally published in magazine form as AMAZING SPIDER-MAN #663-665 and FREE COMIC BOOK DAY 2011 (SPIDER-MAN). First printing 2011. ardcover ISBN# 978-0-7851-5108-1. Softcover ISBN# 978-0-7851-5109-8. Published by MARVEL WORLDWIDE, INC., a subsidiary of MARVEL ENTERTAINMENT, LLC. OFFICE OF PUBLICATION: 135 West 50th Street, ew York, NY 10020. Copyright © 2011 and 2012 Marvel Characters, Inc. All rights reserved. Hardcover: $19.99 per copy in the U.S. and $21.99 in Canada (GST #R127032852). Softcover: $15.99 per copy in the U.S. nd $17.99 in Canada (GST #R127032852). Canadian Agreement #40668537. All characters featured in this issue and the distinctive names and likenesses thereof, and all related indicia are trademarks of Marvel haracters, Inc. No similarity between any of the names, characters, persons, and/or institutions in this magazine with those of any living or dead person or institution is intended, and any such similarity which may xist is purely coincidental. **Printed in the U.S.A.** ALAN FINE, EVP - Office of the President, Marvel Worldwide, Inc. and EVP & CMO Marvel Characters B.V.; DAN BUCKLEY, Publisher & President - Print, Animation & igital Divisions; JOE QUESADA, Chief Creative Officer; JIM SOKOLOWSKI, Chief Operating Officer; DAVID BOGART, SVP of Business Affairs & Talent Management; TOM BREVOORT, SVP of Publishing; C.B. CEBULSKI, VP of Creator & Content Development; DAVID GABRIEL, SVP of Publishing Sales & Circulation; MICHAEL PASCIULLO, SVP of Brand Planning & Communications; JIM O'KEEFE, VP of Operations & Logistics; DAN CARR, xecutive Director of Publishing Technology; SUSAN CRESPI, Editorial Operations Manager; ALEX MORALES, Publishing Operations Manager; STAN LEE, Chairman Emeritus. For information regarding advertising in larvel Comics or on Marvel.com, please contact John Dokes, SVP Integrated Sales and Marketing, at jdokes@marvel.com. For Marvel subscription inquiries, please call 800-217-9158. **Manufactured between /22/2011 and 9/19/2011 (hardcover), and 8/22/2011 and 3/19/2012 (softcover), by R.R. DONNELLEY, INC., SALEM, VA, USA.**

0 9 8 7 6 5 4 3 2 1

FREE COMIC BOOK DAY 2011 (SPIDER-MAN)
COVER BY HUMBERTO RAMOS & EDGAR DELGADO

While attending a demonstration in radiology, high school student Peter Parker was bitten by a spider which had accidentally been exposed to radioactive rays. Through a miracle of science, Peter soon found that he had gained the spider's powers... and had, in effect, become a human spider! From that day on he was...

the AMAZING SPIDER-MAN

THE WAY OF THE SPIDER

I AM JULIA CARPENTER, THE LATEST PSYCHIC TO CALL HERSELF MADAME WEB. AND IT'S MY GIFT TO SEE THIS...
...THE GREAT WEB OF LIFE WHICH WE ALL WEAVE AS WE CRAWL FROM THE CRADLE TO THE GRAVE.
AND NO SOUL HAS BEEN MORE TIED TO IT THAN...
"PETER"?
ALWAYS LIKED THE NAME "BEN," MYSELF.
THEN "PETER BENJAMIN PARKER" IT IS.
OH, BEN!
"BUT WHERE DOES PETER'S THREAD BEGIN? WITH THE PARENTS WHO BROUGHT HIM INTO THE WORLD?
"OR THE AUNT AND UNCLE WHO RAISED HIM AS THEIR OWN?
I COOKED YOUR FAVORITE BREAKFAST, PETEY-- WHEAT CAKES!
DON'T FATTEN HIM UP TOO MUCH, DEAR. I CAN HARDLY OUTWRESTLE HIM NOW!
"...A SPIDER STRUCK DOWN BY RADIOACTIVE RAYS, THAT WITH ITS LAST BITE...
"...TRANSFERRED ITS AMAZING POWERS TO YOUNG PARKER.
"I THINK HIS STORY TRULY STARTED HERE. WHERE THE THREAD OF HIS UNCLE'S LIFE WAS CUT SHORT...

"OR PERHAPS IT STARTS WITH A *LITERAL* STRAND...
"...FROM AN ERRANT *SPIDER* AT A SCIENCE EXHIBIT...
"POWERS HE SELFISHLY USED IN PURSUIT OF PERSONAL GAIN.
"TILL ONE DAY, WHILE FULL OF HIMSELF AND FAR ABOVE THE AFFAIRS OF OTHERS...
"HE STOOD BY AND DID NOTHING WHILE...
STOP! THIEF!
I OUGHTA RUN YOU IN!
SAVE YOUR BREATH, BUDDY. I'VE GOT THINGS TO DO.
"...BY THE THIEF PETER *COULD* HAVE STOPPED EARLIER.
FOR IT WAS THEN THAT PETER LEARNED HIS GREATEST LESSON...
THAT WITH GREAT *POWER* THERE MUST ALSO COME GREAT *RESPONSIBILITY*.
BUT WHAT IF THERE CAME A TIME WHEN HIS POWER WAS *NOT* SO GREAT?

Now.
FIFTH AVENUE, THE MOST EXPENSIVE SHOPPING DISTRICT IN THE WORLD.*
OW! SO I FIGURED, HEY, I'M EARNING THE BIG BUCKS NOW. MY AUNT'S BIRTHDAY IS COMING UP...
WHY NOT FINALLY BUY HER SOMETHING FROM ONE OF YOUR SWANKIER STORES?
VENOM BLAST!
ZZZAK
ARGH...
PAINFUL UTTERANCE!
SEE, JESS? IT SOUNDS STUPID WHEN YOU CALL STUFF OUT LIKE THAT. JUST SAYIN'.
NEW YORK
3086 A
*WHICH MEANS WE'VE NEVER ACTUALLY SHOPPED THERE.--DAN AND HUMBERTO

LAST THING I EXPECTED WAS STOPPING A ROBBERY--
KTAM
WAIT. LET ME FINISH. (I KNOW, I'M SPIDER-MAN, I STOP ROBBERIES ALL THE TIME).
THIS IS THAT PLAYFUL-BANTER THING YOU ALWAYS DO, ISN'T IT?
I HATE THAT.
GNHH!
DULY NOTED.
I MEANT STOPPING ONE BEING COMMITTED BY HER. SPIDER-WOMAN. A FELLOW AVENGER!
ONE WAY
5 AV
THOK
OOF! SO WHY IS EVERYONE'S FAVORITE SPIDER-FEMME KNOCKING OVER TIFFANY'S?
THAT'D BE HIS FAULT.
THE PRIMATE IN THAT TWO THOUSAND DOLLAR ARMANI.
THE MANDRILL.
NOT YOUR ORDINARY TALKING MONKEY-MAN. HE'S GOT A SUPER-POWER TOO.
HEH.
AMPED-UP PHEROMONES THAT--I'M NOT JOKING--LET HIM CONTROL ALL WOMEN.

THESE TRINKETS BORE ME NOW. I SAY WE WATCH THE END OF THE FIGHT...
...AND THEN GET SOME GELATO.
OOH! WHATEVER YOU SAY, BOSS.
WOULD IT BE HORRIBLY UN-P.C. OF ME TO SAY THAT'S AN AWESOME SUPER-POWER?
JUST LOOK AT HIM! HE'S GOT AN ARMY OF SUPERMODELS!
AND MY PAL, JESSICA HERE.
SPIDER-WOMAN'S GOT ENHANCED PHEROMONES OF HER OWN.
5383
HEY! YOU MOVED! DON'T YOU KNOW THE RULES OF SUPER-HERO-MIND-CONTROL FIGHTS?
YOU'RE SUPPOSED TO BE SLOW AND SLUGGISH! IT'S IN THE HANDBOOK.
PROBLEM IS-- SOMEHOW THAT'S MADE HER MORE SUSCEPTIBLE TO MANDRILL'S ATTACKS!
TSCH. FOR ME...
...THIS IS SLOW AND SLUGGISH.
KEE-RAK
AHH!
STOP IT! I NEED THIS HEAD! I USE IT TO WEAR HATS!
TELL ME. IS THIS WHY YOU BROUGHT ME HERE? TO WATCH THESE HEROES DO BATTLE?
YES. SO, SHANG-CHI? WHAT DO YOU THINK?
I THINK SPIDER-MAN'S MY FRIEND AND I SHOULD GO DOWN THERE AND HELP HIM.
YOU MUSTN'T.

SO YOU KNEW THIS FIGHT WOULD TAKE PLACE AT *THIS* POINT IN TIME?
YES. I'M MADAME WEB. I PREDICTED IT.
AND IT IS IMPORTANT THAT *I* BE HERE AS WELL--BUT *NOT* TO OFFER ASSISTANCE?
CORRECT. YOUR *PRESENCE* HERE IS PIVOTAL.
THERE'S A CHOICE TO BE MADE HERE TODAY, BUT IT'S FOR SPIDER-MAN AND SPIDER-MAN ALONE.
NOW TELL ME, AS THE MASTER OF KUNG FU, WHAT DO YOU MAKE OF THEM?
HER FORM IS EXCELLENT...
"SIGNS OF MILITARY TRAINING. TECHNIQUES USED BY BOTH HYDRA AND S.H.I.E.L.D.
"HER OPPONENT, SPIDER-MAN, ON THE OTHER HAND...
WAKK
"...STILL HAS A *LOT* TO LEARN."
NEW YORK
7125A

YES. FOR YEARS HE RELIED ON HIS SPIDER-SENSE TO GET BY, BUT THAT'S GONE NOW.*
ALL OF HIS PRECOGNITIVE ABILITIES, HIS TIES TO THE "WEB OF LIFE," HAVE BEEN SEVERED.
*BACK IN ASM #654. --SIMPERIN' STEVE.
"AND THOUGH HE USES HIS WITS AND OTHER SKILLS TO COMPENSATE...
VOICE COMMAND: WEB BARRAGE.
FULL SPREAD!
THWIP
THWIP
THWIP
"...IN THE DAYS TO COME...
"...THEY WILL NOT BE ENOUGH.
"IF HE'S TO HAVE ANY CHANCE...
"...OF SURVIVING HIS NEXT GREAT CHALLENGE..."
...HE MUST REINVENT HIMSELF.
HE MUST BECOME A WARRIOR.
IT WOULD BE MY HONOR TO INSTRUCT HIM IN THE WAYS OF--
NO. AGAIN, THAT CHOICE IS NOT FOR YOU TO MAKE.

WUMP
YES! SEE THAT? TOOK SOME DOING, BUT I FINALLY...
SPIDEY HIT A GIRL!
WOTTA CREEP!
NYC TAXI
5L57
ADC 6274
OH, CUT ME SOME SLACK! THIS'S SPIDER-WOMAN! SHE'S TOUGH, MAN. AND SHE'S...
...TOTALLY SHRUGGING THAT OFF.
CUTE. MY TURN.
HA!
GEEZ, THIS'S TAKIN' FOREVER. I THOUGHT WE WERE GETTING GELATO.
OF COURSE, DEAR. SPIDER-WOMAN, BE A DOLL, WRAP THIS UP AND KILL THE PEST.
POW
UNHH...
CAN'T GET CLOSE ENOUGH TO MANDRILL, AND CAN'T TAKE OUT JESS-- EVEN IF I WANTED TO.
FACE IT, SPIDEY, THIS STINKS.
WAIT! THAT'S IT!

BENDEL
HENRI BENDEL
I'M ALL OVER THIS! BUT FIRST-- AH! THERE WE GO.
WHEN I WAS SHOPPING FOR AUNT MAY EARLIER...
...THAT STORE HAD EXACTLY WHAT I NEED!
SCUSI!
HEY! YOU CAN'T GO INTO OUR FINE ESTABLISHMENT LIKE DAT!
MAN'S GOTTA POINT. I REALLY SHOULD ACCESSORIZE.
YOU HAVE ANYTHING HERE THAT GOES WITH A WEB MOTIF?
NOTIONS AND SUNDRIES, THIRD FLOOR.
NOW THAT'S SERVICE.
GET BACK HERE, SPIDER! YOU HEARD THE MANDRILL!
TIME TO DIE!
HOLD IT! YOU CAN'T--
AHH!
KSHH!

C'MON! C'MON! C'MON!
IT'S AROUND HERE SOMEWHERE...
BINGO!
THIS'S THE RIGHT SECTION.
NOW I JUST NEED A SECOND BEFORE SPIDER-WOMAN SHOWS HER--
ZKAM

KE-RECHHHKSHHH
OWWW!
OH, SPIDER-SENSE, I MISS YOU SO MU-HUH-HUCH.
WELL, THAT GOT ME WHERE I WANTED TO GO. WAS JUST HOPING TO GET HERE A LITTLE MORE GRACEFUL--

EEP!
JESS? SNAP OUT IT. WE'RE FRIENDS, REMEMBER?
MANDRILL WANTS YOU DEAD. THAT'S ALL THAT COUNTS.

DOESN'T MATTER HOW CLOSE WE--
≠SNIFF≠-- CLOSE WE ARE--
OH, MY GOD...YOU REEK!
A DOZEN BOTTLES OF PERFUME. MY NEW SIGNATURE SCENT. I CALL IT: Distraction.
JESS? THAT THE REAL YOU?
YEAH, I'M BACK. NOW THAT YOU GOT THE SMELL OF MANDRILL OUT OF MY NOSE.
WELL, YOU KNOW THE RULE ABOUT FIGHTING MONKEY-MEN. SEE NO EVIL, HEAR NO EVIL, SMELL NO EVIL.
SPEAK NO EVIL.
RIGHT. AND SPEAKING OF EVIL MONKEYS...
THIS WAY, DARLINGS. WE'LL HAVE A NOSH AND THEN HIT F.A.O. SCHWARZ
YES, MASTER.
SUPERMODELS. WHAT WAS I THINKING? WITH THOSE STICK FIGURE ARMS YOU CAN BARELY CARRY ANYTHING.
NEXT TIME? AEROBICS INSTRUCTORS. OR PRO WRESTLERS. DEFINITELY GALS WITH MORE MEAT ON THEIR BONES...
≠SNIFF≠ UGH. WHAT'S THAT SMELL?
TAP TAP
YOU RANG?

THAT, SIR, IS THE SWEET BOUQUET OF--
--JUSTICE!
WHAM!
OOH-OOH-AHH!

Later...
NEW YORK HOT DOGS
I'VE NEVER FELT MORE DEGRADED IN MY LIFE.
AND I'VE BEEN ON HOWARD STERN!
YOU'LL BE HEARING FROM MY ATTORNEY, CREEP!
TAKE HIM AWAY, BOYS.
AND SHE DOES MEAN "BOYS." WE'RE SERIOUS!
NO FEMALE OFFICERS ANYWHERE NEAR MR. AXE-BODY WASH THERE! COMPRENDE?
THE RAFT
IT'S OKAY. HE'S GOT A POWER INHIBITOR COLLAR ON.
HOW MANY TIMES HAVE I HEARD THAT ONE?
UH, LOU? WHAT'RE WE SUPPOSED TO DO ABOUT SPIDEY? ISN'T HE A VIGILANTE OR SOMETHING? SHOULD WE ARREST HIM?
YEAH... I'M NOT SURE.
YOU STILL HAVE TO DEAL WITH THIS?
I KNOW.
GUYS, DON'T KNOW IF YOU'VE HEARD, BUT...
I'M ONE OF THE MIGHTY AVENGERS
YEAH. HE IS, AIN'T HE? WITH CAP AND THOR AND WHATNOT.
GUESS THAT ANSWERS THAT.
HM. IT ACTUALLY WORKED.
WHATTYA KNOW...
THAT'S THEM!

THEY'RE THE ONES, BOSS! THE HOOLIGANS WHO SMASHED UP OUR FINE ESTABLISHMENT.
ALL RIGHT! AND WHO'S GOING TO PAY FOR ALL THAT DAMAGE?!
UM... SEND THE BILL TO TONY STARK.
YOU CAN DO THAT?
I'M AN AVENGER
ESCAD
OH. OKAY THEN.
WELL, ON THAT NOTE...SEE YOU AROUND, SPIDEY.
LATER, JESS. AND NEXT TIME... I WON'T GO SO EASY ON YA.
HI THERE. ONE DOG WITH ALL THE WORKS PLEASE.
FIVE BUCKS.
AHEM I'M AN AVENGER
YEAH? AVENGE THIS!
AH, WELL. WAS GOOD WHILE IT LASTED.
GOOD FOR NOTHING PIECE OF--
SPIDER-MAN!

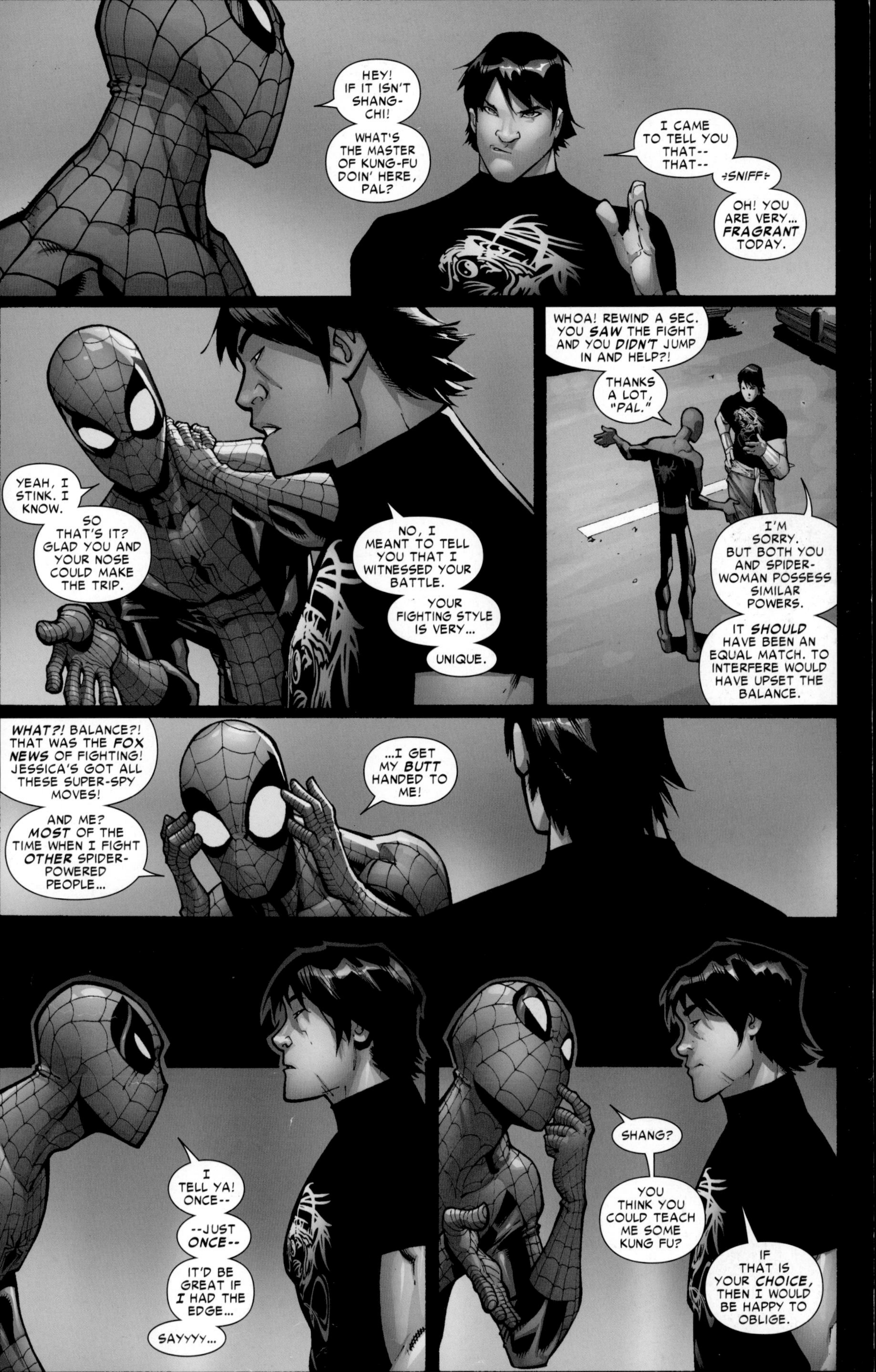
HEY! IF IT ISN'T SHANG-CHI!
WHAT'S THE MASTER OF KUNG-FU DOIN' HERE, PAL?
I CAME TO TELL YOU THAT-- THAT--
SNIFF
OH! YOU ARE VERY... FRAGRANT TODAY.
YEAH, I STINK. I KNOW.
SO THAT'S IT? GLAD YOU AND YOUR NOSE COULD MAKE THE TRIP.
NO, I MEANT TO TELL YOU THAT I WITNESSED YOUR BATTLE.
YOUR FIGHTING STYLE IS VERY...
UNIQUE.
WHOA! REWIND A SEC. YOU SAW THE FIGHT AND YOU DIDN'T JUMP IN AND HELP?!
THANKS A LOT, "PAL."
I'M SORRY. BUT BOTH YOU AND SPIDER-WOMAN POSSESS SIMILAR POWERS.
IT SHOULD HAVE BEEN AN EQUAL MATCH. TO INTERFERE WOULD HAVE UPSET THE BALANCE.
WHAT?! BALANCE?! THAT WAS THE FOX NEWS OF FIGHTING! JESSICA'S GOT ALL THESE SUPER-SPY MOVES!
AND ME? MOST OF THE TIME WHEN I FIGHT OTHER SPIDER-POWERED PEOPLE...
...I GET MY BUTT HANDED TO ME!
I TELL YA! ONCE--
--JUST ONCE--
IT'D BE GREAT IF I HAD THE EDGE...
SAYYYY...
SHANG?
YOU THINK YOU COULD TEACH ME SOME KUNG FU?
IF THAT IS YOUR CHOICE, THEN I WOULD BE HAPPY TO OBLIGE.

The Next Day...
CROTON-ON-HUDSON, NEW YORK. AN ABANDONED HAI-DAI TRAINING FACILITY.
ONE HUNDRED HAI-DAI WARRIORS WERE INSTRUCTED HERE-- IN THE DEADLIEST OF ARTS...
...SO THAT THEY COULD SERVE MY FATHER, ZHENG ZU, IN HIS CRIMINAL EMPIRE.
NOW, TO RESTORE THE BALANCE...
...YOU MUST EXCEL A HUNDRED-FOLD.
NO SWEAT. I MEAN, I'VE GOT SPIDER-STRENGTH AND SPEED. I'M ALREADY AHEAD OF THE GAME, RIGHT?
WRONG. THIS INHIBITOR COLLAR WILL KEEP THOSE POWERS IN CHECK.
BEFORE I TRAIN THE SPIDER, FIRST I MUST TRAIN THE MAN.
WHOA. INHIBITOR COLLARS ARE HARD TO COME BY. HOW'D YOU SCORE IT?
WHEN I EXPLAINED WHAT WE WERE DOING TO THE AVENGERS, AND THAT IT WOULD MOST LIKELY INVOLVE PHYSICAL PAIN...
...TONY STARK WAS MORE THAN HAPPY TO DONATE IT.
IT WAS THE HOT DOG, WASN'T IT? SHOULDN'T'VE TRIED TO CHARGE HIM FOR THE HOT DOG.
NO MORE JOKES.
WE DO THIS SERIOUSLY OR NOT AT ALL.
YES.
THEN LET'S BEGIN.

In The Weeks That Follow...
GOOD! THAT IS THE CORRECT FORM.
NOW YOU NEED TO HONE IT. REPEAT IT. PRACTICE IT A THOUSAND TIMES IF YOU CAN.
NOT A PROBLEM, SHANG. ONE OF THE BENEFITS OF OUR LINE OF WORK IS...
"...THIS IS NO MERE APPLICATION OF BRUTE FORCE."
"...AND LEARN WHAT HE HAS TO TEACH YOU...
"...WHILE THERE IS STILL TIME.

...YOU ALWAYS GET PLENTY OF SPARRING PARTNERS.
THINK I'VE GOT THIS. IT'S MASS, ACCELERATION, LEVERAGE, AND A KNOWLEDGE OF HUMAN BIOLOGY.
THAT'S SCIENCE. AND I'M *GREAT* AT SCIENCE.
NO, SPIDER-MAN, IT IS SO MUCH MORE...
IT IS AN ART.
AND AN EXPRESSION OF THE SELF.
WHAT IF MOST OF MYSELF IS SCIENCE?
STOP FIGHTING HIM, SPIDER.
THE WEB'S TIGHTENING. YOU HAVE TO HURRY...
YOU'VE DONE WELL. IT'S TIME TO REMOVE THE COLLAR.
SO I GUESS THAT'S IT, HUH? WE DONE?
NO. WE ARE NOW HALF WAY.
HALF WAY?!
YES. NOW WE MUST FIND YOUR OWN FORM OF MARTIAL ARTS. ONE BASED AROUND ALL OF YOUR SPECIAL ABILITIES.
FROM THIS POINT ON, YOU SHALL LEARN *THE WAY OF THE SPIDER!*

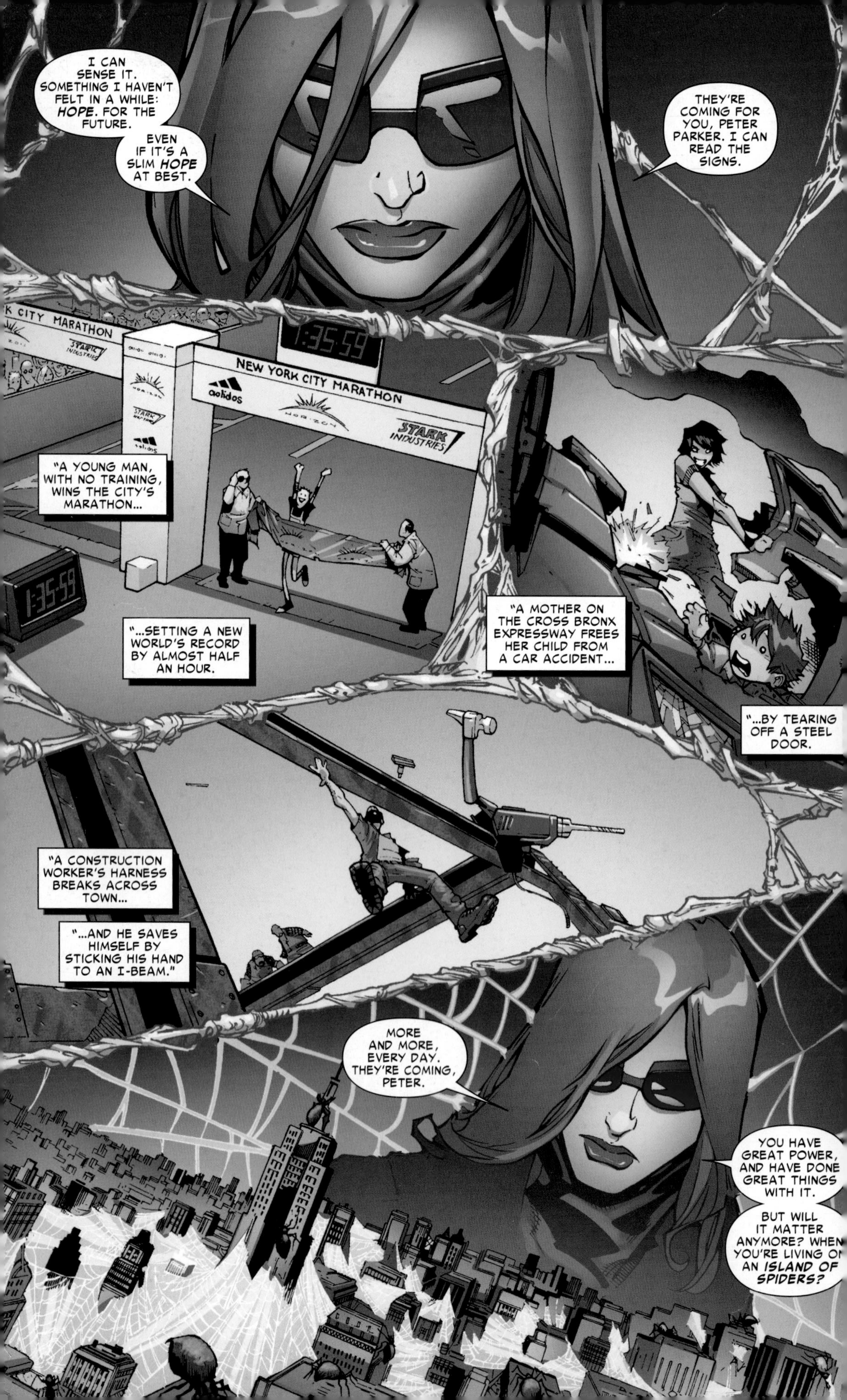

I CAN SENSE IT. SOMETHING I HAVEN'T FELT IN A WHILE: *HOPE*. FOR THE FUTURE.
EVEN IF IT'S A SLIM *HOPE* AT BEST.
THEY'RE COMING FOR YOU, PETER PARKER. I CAN READ THE SIGNS.
NEW YORK CITY MARATHON
adidos
HOR-ZON
STARK INDUSTRIES
1:35:59
"A YOUNG MAN, WITH NO TRAINING, WINS THE CITY'S MARATHON...
"...SETTING A NEW WORLD'S RECORD BY ALMOST HALF AN HOUR.
"A MOTHER ON THE CROSS BRONX EXPRESSWAY FREES HER CHILD FROM A CAR ACCIDENT...
"...BY TEARING OFF A STEEL DOOR.
"A CONSTRUCTION WORKER'S HARNESS BREAKS ACROSS TOWN...
"...AND HE SAVES HIMSELF BY STICKING HIS HAND TO AN I-BEAM."
MORE AND MORE, EVERY DAY. THEY'RE COMING, PETER.
YOU HAVE GREAT POWER, AND HAVE DONE GREAT THINGS WITH IT.
BUT WILL IT MATTER ANYMORE? WHEN YOU'RE LIVING ON AN *ISLAND OF SPIDERS?*

AMAZING SPIDER-MAN #663

DAILY BUGLE

TOP STORY

WRAITH TERRORIZES UNDERWORLD

By BEN URICH, Editor In Chief

The NYPD has been baffled to arrive at a string of drug-related crime scenes to find the perpetrators more than willing to confess, as long as they are thrown in jail where SHE can't get them... (see full story)

F.E.A.S.T. CENTER SAVES LIVES

Martin Li's F.E.A.S.T. Center continues to offer Food, Emergency Aid, Shelter and Training to the people of New York. Devoted volunteers have been working tirelessly to prepare for the semi-annual food drive...

INVENTIONS ON THE HORIZON

Peter Parker has been earning his keep as the most recent new scientist at Horizon Labs with a string of inventions ... (see full story)

(Pictured: Horizon founder Max Modell with Parker, and fellow Horizon scientists Uatu Jackson and Bella Fishbach.)

VIRAL VIDEO

FALLEN HEROES REMEMBERED

The NYPD remembers brave officers who lost their lives in the line of duty (click to see in memoriam video)

ueens.
ast River
Vaterfront.
MY NAME IS EDDIE BROCK.
IN ANOTHER LIFE, I WAS CAST IN SHADOW--AND NOTHING MORE THAN A MONSTER.
BUT FATE HAD A HIGHER CALLING FOR ME. I'VE BEEN REBORN AS THE LIGHT WHICH WILL LEAD YOU ALL OUT OF DARKNESS.
FOR ALL THE POISONS THAT PLAGUE THIS EARTH, I AM YOUR
ANTI-VENOM
AND I ALONE KNOW YOUR CITY'S DARKEST SECRET...
...THAT ITS GREATEST SINNER, THE CRIME LORD MR. NEGATIVE...
...IS ALSO ITS GREATEST SAINT, THE BELOVED PHILANTHROPIST, MARTIN LI.
YOU'D NEVER BELIEVE ME, THOUGH. NOT WITH MY PAST.
SO THERE'S NOTHING LEFT TO DO BUT TAKE DOWN HIS CRIMINAL EMPIRE ONE PIECE AT A TIME.
LIKE TONIGHT, AND THIS OPIUM SHIPMENT I'VE CAUGHT WIND OF...
PAK
PKOW

CAN'T SEE! IS SHE STILL THERE?!
PAKK
KEEP FIRING!
PKOW
WHAT ABOUT THE OTHERS?
@#$* THEM!
WHAT ABOUT THE DELIVERY?
@#$* THAT TOO!
NEGATIVE'S FOOT SOLDIERS. TIME TO SHOW THEM WHAT THEY'RE UP AGAINST!

CRIMINALS, BEWARE! YOU'RE A DISEASE AND I'M THE CURE! I AM--
HEY!
OUTTA THE WAY!

GET BACK HERE!
FORTUNA

I SAID YOU'RE THE--
AH! LET GO OF ME! SHE'S AFTER US!
WHAT'RE YOU TALKING ABOUT?! SHE?!

BRTT
BRRT
YOUR GUNS WON'T HELP YOU.
STAY BACK!
BEGGING FOR YOUR LIFE WON'T HELP YOU.
WHY-- WHY WON'T YOU DIE?!
DON'T YOU KNOW?
I'M THE WRAITH. AND I'M ALREADY DEAD.
AHH! GOD, DON'T KILL ME!!
GOD? GOD WON'T HELP YOU EITHER. AND DEATH?
DEATH WILL HELP YOU LEAST OF ALL. THERE'S NO ESCAPE.
KLUNG
NOT FOR YOU, RONNIE CHIN.

OH, THERE ARE SPECIAL CIRCLES OF HELL WAITING FOR MEN LIKE YOU, RONNIE.
THOSE WITH *FAR* TOO MANY SINS TO CONFESS.
THE HOUSE YOU BURNED DOWN.
THE YOUNG MAN YOU THREW OFF THE TRAIN.
THE WOMAN YOU BURIED ALIVE...
HOW-- HOW DO YOU KNOW ABOUT...?
ONLY *ONE* THING WILL SAVE YOU. TELL ME, HOW IS NEGATIVE GETTING HIS SHIPMENTS PAST THE AUTHORITIES? WHO'S HIS INSIDE MAN?
HE'D KILL ME!
YES. BUT I CAN DO *FAR* WORSE.
WHO ARE YOU?!
YOU WANT TO KNOW?
HA HA HA HA!
HERE. I'LL SHOW YOU...

"THE WRAITH"?
SHE-- SHE'S EVERYWHERE, MAN!
AND YOU'RE MORE SCARED OF HER...
...THAN ME?!

IDIOT!
SPAASH

HRM.
NOW THIS, I GOTTA SEE.

ALL RIGHT, SO WHAT'S THE BIG--
NO. IT CAN'T BE.
I KNOW YOU.

The Return Of Anti-Venom
YOU'RE JEAN DeWOLFF?!
Part One: The Ghost of Jean DeWolff

I GOT EVERYTHING I NEEDED HERE.
BUT YOU'RE SUPPOSED TO BE...
WASHH
...DEAD?
Y-YOU SENT HER AWAY?
WHOEVER YOU ARE-- THANK YOU, MAN! YOU SAVED ME!
UNBELIEVABLE.
"SHH...BACK TO BED. THIS'S ALL JUST A DREAM."

Tribeca.
THE APARTMENT OF PETER PARKER...
NAH. IT'S OKAY, CARLIE. I'M UP.
SORRY. DIDN'T MEAN TO WAKE YOU. YOU CAME IN SO LATE LAST NIGHT, AND--BOOM--OUT LIKE A LIGHT.
THOUGHT YOU COULD USE THE SLEEP.
I WANT YOU TO KNOW I'M PROUD OF YOU, PETE. THE WAY YOU'RE WORKING SO HARD.
YOU MUST REALLY BE GETTING A LOT DONE FOR YOUR BOSS AT HORIZON.
YEAH. YOU KNOW IT.
EXCEPT I'M NOT.
BEEN SPENDING ALMOST ALL MY TIME AS SPIDEY LATELY. HOW CAN'T I? I'M ON TWO SUPER HERO TEAMS AT THE SAME TIME:
THE AVENGERS AND THE FF!
AND PATROLLING THE STREETS AT NIGHT. EVER SINCE I LET MARLA JAMESON DIE, I'VE BEEN PUSHING MYSELF.
TRYING TO BE THE BEST SPIDER-MAN I CAN BE. DOING EVERYTHING THAT'S BEEN ASKED OF ME AND MORE.
I CAN DO THIS! JUST HAVE TO BE SURE I STAY ON TOP OF THINGS AS PETE. LIKE MAKING TIME FOR CARLIE...
SO? WHERE ARE YOU GOING? WANT TO HANG OUT?
NO CAN DO, SIR. DUTY CALLS. CAPTAIN WATANABE NEEDS ME AT A CRIME SCENE.
NYPD
WELL, MORE LIKE A FOILED CRIME SCENE. LOOKS LIKE THE WRAITH HAS STRUCK AGAIN.
THE WRAITH?
MYSTERIOUS VIGILANTE... FROM BEYOND THE GRAAAVE! OO-OOH!
NIIICE.
NOW DO YOUR SHE-HULK.

A NEW VIGILANTE IN TOWN? AND USING THE LATE BRIAN DEWOLFF'S ALTER-EGO NO LESS. BETTER ADD THAT TO THE LIST.
ONE MORE THING TO CHECK OUT AS SPIDEY...IN ALL OF MY "FREE TIME."
HAVE FUN.
ALWAYS. Y'KNOW ME. I LIVE FOR THIS STUFF. OH, AND HONEY, BEFORE I FORGET...
...CONGRATULATIONS!
NYPD

WHAT DO YOU MEAN...?
WAIT. WITH EVERYTHING THAT'S BEEN GOING ON, I TOTALLY FORGOT.
THAT IS TODAY, ISN'T IT?

SERIOUSLY, THIS IS A MAJOR TURNING POINT IN THE LIFE OF ONE PETER BENJAMIN PARKER...
...AND IT COMPLETELY SLIPPED MY MIND.
HORIZON
WELL, THAT SETTLES IT. I HAVE TO PUT IN SOME TIME AT HORIZON LABS NOW. BECAUSE WITHOUT THIS JOB...

...I'D NEVER HAVE A DAY LIKE TODAY.
HEY GUYS, WHAT'S GOIN' ON?
PLEASE, PARKER. LIKE YOU WEREN'T DROPPING IN--JUST TO RUB OUR NOSES IN IT?
SAJANI, CHILL. LIKE IT HASN'T HAPPENED TO YOU THREE TIMES.

SMEK
I'M WITH GRADY. WAY TO GO, PETE.
C'MON, DUDE. SCIENCE HIGH FIVE!
THANKS, GRADY. THIS ISN'T DORKY AT ALL.
IS MAX AROUND?

"YEAH. HE'S IN UATU'S LAB, HELPING HIM WITH HIS S.I.S.* APP."
I LIKE THIS NEW DELIVERY SYSTEM YOU'VE DESIGNED. IT'S MORE PORTABLE THAN OUR E-READER.
THAT'S A MARK 2. FOR MARK 3, I WANNA GET IT DOWN TO A CONTACT LENS AND AN EARBUD...
UATU. MR. MODELL. WHAT'S UP?
*SUSPECT IDENTIFICATION SOFTWARE. AS SEEN IN ASM #656.--STEVE.
LOOK WHO FINALLY DECIDED TO SHOW UP.
I HOPE, FOR YOUR SAKE, YOU HAVE A NEW PROJECT FOR ME, MR. PARKER.
YOU BET, MAX...
"...MEET ME IN TESTING ROOM THREE, AND I'LL SHOW YOU. PERSONALLY."
VRRRMMMM
FKAMG
CHEAP. EASY TO MASS-PRODUCE. AND TEN TIMES MORE EFFECTIVE THAN ANY HELMET ON THE MARKET.
AND, AT A HIGHER DENSITY, BULLETPROOF?
YEAH.
I SAW FOOTAGE OF SPIDER-MAN WEARING THIS WEEKS AGO. AND YOU'RE TRYING IT ON A DUMMY SECOND?
UM...
WELL, I CAN'T ARGUE WITH RESULTS. GOOD WORK, MR. PARKER. AND YOUR OTHER ACHIEVMENT TODAY? KUDOS. YOU DESERVE IT.

Peter's Private Lab.
WONDER WHAT MAX'D THINK IF HE KNEW THE WHOLE STORY. THAT I DON'T JUST DESIGN TECH FOR MY "FRIEND" SPIDER-MAN...

...I AM MY OWN TEST DUMMY! BUT IT'S LIKE MAX SAID. CAN'T ARGUE WITH RESULTS.
I USED MY STEALTH SUIT TO COME UP WITH ALL-NEW NOISE REDUCTION HEADPHONES...
...MY BULLETPROOF SUIT TO DESIGN A NEW KIND OF MOTORCYCLE HELMET...
...AND FOR MY NEXT TRICK...

...A VOICE ACTIVATION UPGRADE FOR MY WEB-SHOOTERS.

RIGHT SHOOTER: WEB-BARRAGE!
LEFT SHOOTER: WIDE NET!
THWIP-IP-IP
THWOPP

SWEET! BETTER TECH MAKES ME A BETTER SPIDEY. IT MAKES PETE THE BIG BUCKS.
AND THE REST OF THE WORLD GETS HIGH-QUALITY HORIZON MERCHANDISE.
WIN-WIN-WIN.
AND FOR THE FINAL CHERRY ON TOP OF THE ICE CREAM SUNDAE THAT IS MY LIFE...

AS OF TODAY, WEALTH AND FAME...
...ARE MY REWARD!

WHO IS HE?
AMERICAN SCIENCE JOURNAL
DAILY BUGLE
HERC VERSUS HOBBY
The Greek God and the Goblin battle in Brooklyn.
Newstime
WHATEVER HAPPENED TO DAREDEVIL?
MARTIN LI DON TES MILLIONS TO MU EUM
MARTIN LI DONATES MILLIONS TO MU EUM

THWIP
DAILY BUGLE
HERC VERSUS
The Greek God

THWAP
DAILY BUGLE
HERC VERSUS
The Greek God and the Goblin

STAY CALM.
(LIKE I HAVEN'T WANTED THIS SINCE I WAS EIGHT...)

FLIPPING.
FLIPPING.
SO MANY SUBSCRIPTION CARDS.
cloning's future
AMERICAN SCIENCE JOURNAL

BINGO!
EXT FRONTIER
CROMOLECULA
CHEMISTRY
r Parker, project lead
rizon Laboratory's Rese
Development Division, o
eation of his revolution
impact resisting polyme

YES!
CHECK IT OUT!
PUBLISHED!
IN THE AMERICAN SCIENCE JOURNAL!
FORGET THE AVENGERS, THE FF, SPIDER-POWERS...
...AND TWELVE ZILLION FRONT PAGE PHOTOS IN THE DAILY BUGLE! YOU CAN KEEP 'EM ALL!
I DID THIS! ALL ON MY OWN! WITH MY BIG OL' BRAIN!
YEAH!
cloning's future
AMERICAN SCIENCE JOURNAL

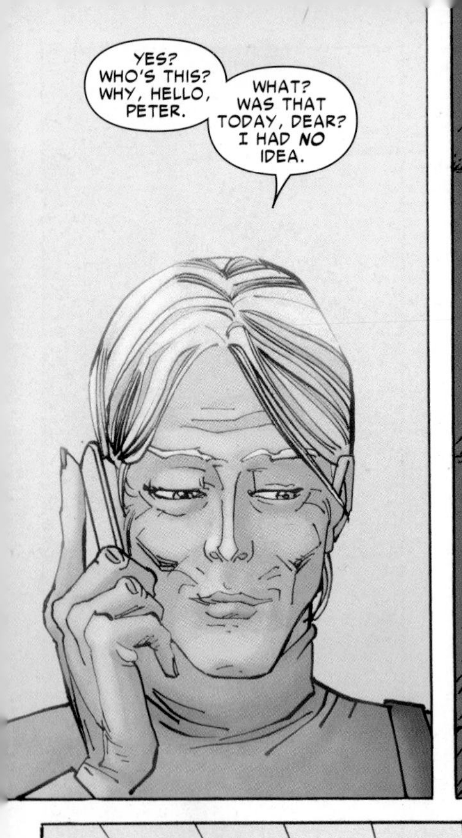
YES? WHO'S THIS? WHY, HELLO, PETER.
WHAT? WAS THAT TODAY, DEAR? I HAD NO IDEA.

YEAH, AUNT MAY. JUST CAME OUT. THE JUNE ISSUE. AMERICAN SCIENCE JOURNAL. PAGE EIGHTEEN.
NO. THE AMERICAN SCIENCE JOURNAL. YOU KNOW. YOU RENEWED MY SUBSCRIPTION EVERY CHRISTMAS? YES, THAT ONE.
IT'S...UH... KIND OF A BIG THING FOR ME. THOUGHT YOU'D WANT TO KNOW.

YOU DON'T SAY?
OH, GIVE ME THAT, YOU MEAN WOMAN.
cloning's future
AMERICAN SCIENCE JOURNAL
cloning's future
AMERICAN SCIENCE JOURNAL

PETER? IT'S JAY. YOUR AUNT'S PUTTING YOU ON. SHE HAD A CRATE OF 'EM SENT OVER.
WE WORKED A SHIFT AT THE F.E.A.S.T. SHELTER, AND NOW SHE'S PASSING OUT COPIES TO EVERYONE.
PAGE EIGHTEEN, ESTHER.
YOU MUST BE SO PROUD!

HI THERE. HAVE WE MET BEFORE?
IT'S PROBABLY THE BEARD, MRS. PARKER. THAT'S WHAT'S NEW.

OH, MY. I GUESS I HAVEN'T BEEN AROUND FOR A WHILE. I GOT MARRIED. IT'S MRS. JAMESON NOW.
I'M HAPPY FOR YOU, MA'AM. YOU'RE GOOD PEOPLE. SO WHAT KEPT YOU AWAY FOR SO LONG?

FOR THE LIFE OF ME, I CAN'T REMEMBER. I-I THINK IT HAD SOMETHING TO DO WITH MR. LI...
FUNNY. FOR ME IT'S THE OTHER WAY 'ROUND.
WHEN I'M HANGIN' AROUND MARTIN LI, I FEEL LIKE I LEARN SOMETHIN' NEW EVERY DAY.
PRIVATE

LOST THE ENTIRE SHIPMENT THIS TIME, BOSS. ALONG WITH THREE MEN.
DON'T TELL ME, IT WAS THE THE WRAITH AGAIN, WASN'T IT?
AND ANTI-VENOM. DON'T KNOW HOW THEY'RE DOING IT.
WHERE ARE THEY GETTING ALL THEIR INFORMATION?

FOR NOW, ALL THAT MATTERS IS THAT THEY ARE GETTING IT. I CAN WORK WITH THAT.
I HAVE A PLAN. BUT ONE I'LL NEED TO IMPLEMENT...

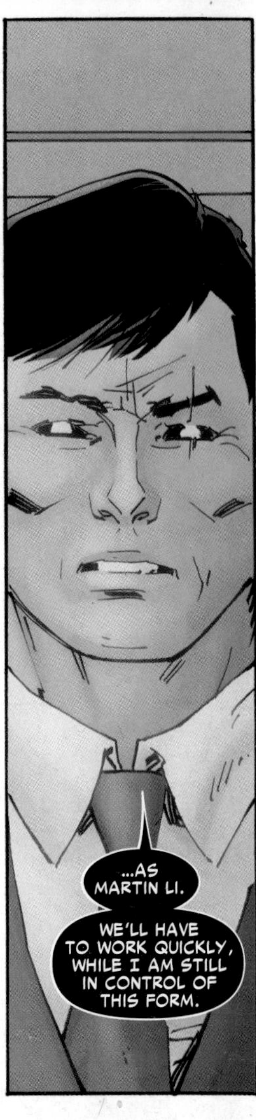
...AS MARTIN LI.
WE'LL HAVE TO WORK QUICKLY, WHILE I AM STILL IN CONTROL OF THIS FORM.

THERE HE IS NOW. THE KIND AND BENEVOLENT MARTIN LI. LOOK AT YOU...
MARTIN?
...USING A HOMELESS SHELTER AS YOUR SECRET BASE OF OPERATIONS.
WELL TWO CAN PLAY THAT GAME.
MAY! IT'S BEEN FAR TOO LONG.
I KNOW, MARTIN! IT SEEMS LIKE THE LAST TIME I SAW YOU WAS--
I CAN EXPLAIN...
SOMETHING'S WRONG HERE. I-I SHOULD TELL SOMEONE...
NO.
YOU SHOULDN'T.
HNGK
OF COURSE, PETER. I'LL PUT HER BACK ON--
MAY!

JAY?! WHAT HAPPENED?
IT'S YOUR AUNT. SHE PASSED OUT. SHE'S NOT--
DON'T WASTE TIME TALKING TO ME!
OF COURSE! I'M HANGING UP AND CALLING AN AMBULANCE!
GOOD! I'M ON MY WAY!

THE F.E.A.S.T. CENTER, ON AVENUE A. PLEASE HURRY!
YES, I'LL STAY ON.
NO. WE HAVE NO IDEA WHAT BROUGHT IT ON.
LIKE HELL WE DON'T. WHAT WAS I THINKING? WAITED TOO LONG.
SHOULD'VE KILLED THE BEAST BY CUTTING OFF ITS HEAD...

"...INSTEAD OF PICKING OFF ITS MEN ONE BY ONE."
ONE MORE TIME, MR. CHIN. JUST SO WE'RE CLEAR. YOU'VE BEEN READ YOUR MIRANDA RIGHTS...
...YOU DO NOT HAVE AN ATTORNEY PRESENT. AND THAT IS ONE LONG LIST OF CRIMES YOU'RE CONFESSING TO.
DON'T YOU GET IT? I HAVE TO WHILE THERE'S STILL TIME! BEFORE SHE COMES BACK.
RIIIGHT. THIS MYSTERIOUS WRAITH.
SHE AIN'T A MYSTERY. SHE'S A GHOST. I SAW HER FACE.

SHE'S--SHE'S THAT DEAD COP FROM WAY BACK. SHOTGUN TO THE CHEST.
THE WOLF. Y'KNOW...JEAN DeWOLFF.
UM. CAPTAIN WATANABE?
NOT NOW, COOPER.
A WORD, PLEASE.

YURI, DON'T KNOW IF YOU REMEMBER...
BACK WHEN MYSTERIO WAS MAKING IT LOOK LIKE PEOPLE WERE COMING BACK FROM THE DEAD*...
ASM #618-620--SW

...JEAN WAS THE NEXT ONE ON HIS LIST.
AND?
HE HAD THE "GAG" READY. THERE WAS A MASK...
...ONLY YOU, ME, AND SPIDER-MAN KNEW ABOUT IT.
YES. IT WAS IN BAD TASTE. I HAD IT DESTROYED.

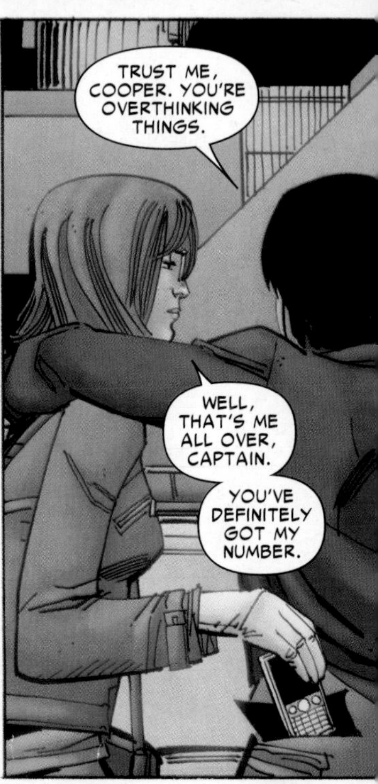
TRUST ME, COOPER. YOU'RE OVERTHINKING THINGS.
WELL, THAT'S ME ALL OVER, CAPTAIN.
YOU'VE DEFINITELY GOT MY NUMBER.

The F.E.A.S.T. Shelter.
JAY?
I'M RIGHT HERE, MAY. I'M GOING TO CALL PETER AND TELL HIM WHICH HOSPITAL WE'LL BE AT.
PLEASE KEEP ME UPDATED, MR. JAMESON. I WANT TO MAKE SURE SHE'S ALL RIGHT.
I'LL BET YOU DO, YOU MONSTER! YOU'LL WANT TO KNOW THE SECOND THAT DEAR, SWEET WOMAN CAN TALK.
I SAW THAT LOOK ON HER FACE. SHE KNOWS YOUR SECRET TOO!
FDNY
FDNY EMT
WHAT WILL YOU DO NOW?
COME. WE'VE WASTED ENOUGH TIME ON THIS... DISTRACTION.
THERE'S WORK TO DO.
ALL THIS TIME, I LAID IN WAIT AND THOUGHT MYSELF SO CLEVER.
AND NOW, ONE OF THE KINDEST PEOPLE I'VE EVER KNOWN MIGHT PAY THE PRICE!

ENOUGH!
THIS ENDS RIGHT HERE! RIGHT NOW!

MARTIN LI!
YOU'RE A MALIGNANCY.

RUNCH
A CANCER ON THE WORLD!

AND I'M HERE TO CUT YOU OUT!
KRANG
BOSS! IT'S BROCK! CAN YOU--?
NO! I CAN'T CHANGE. IT'S TOO SOON. I'M STUCK AS LI!
I'M POWERLESS, DAMN IT!

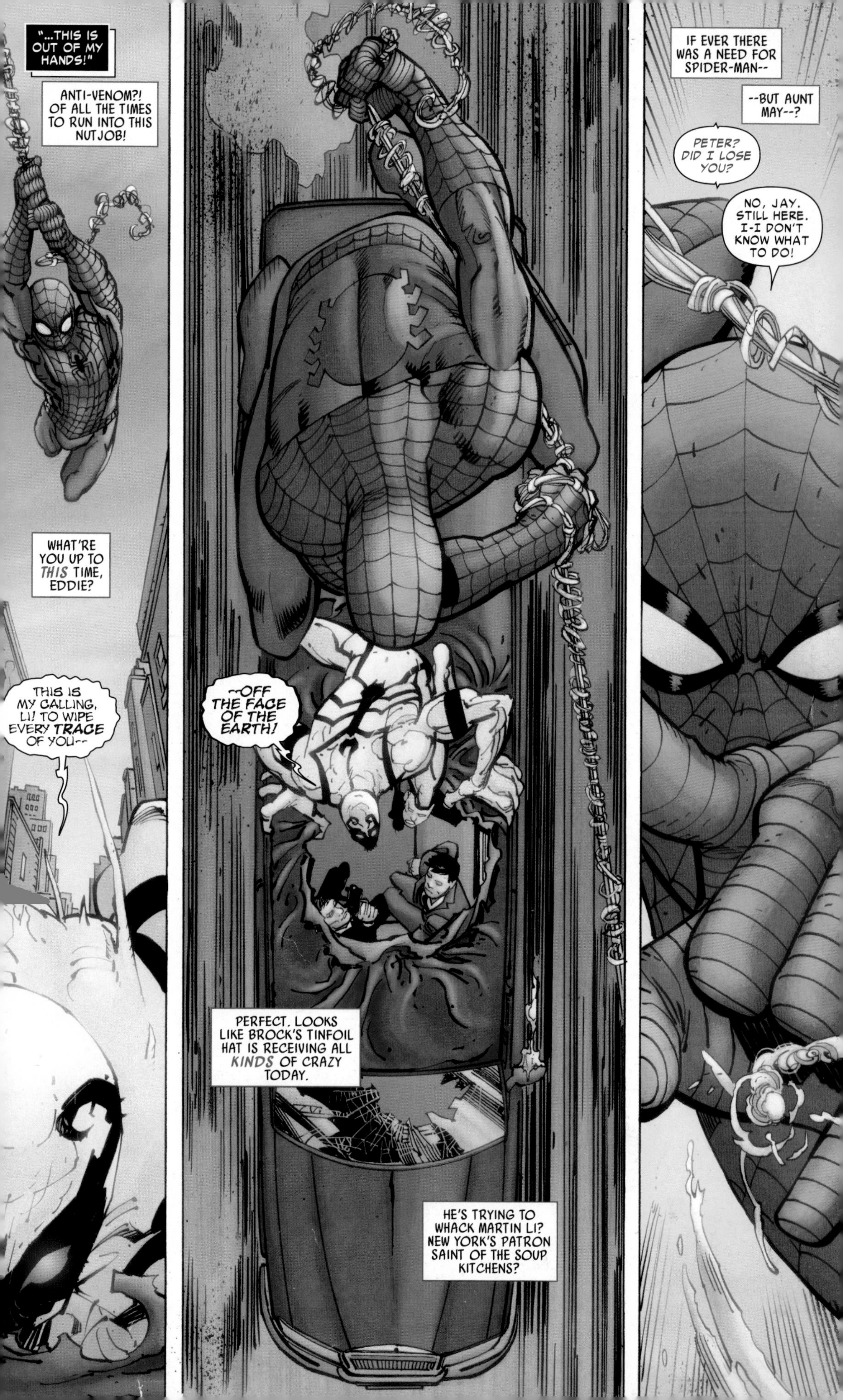
"...THIS IS OUT OF MY HANDS!"
ANTI-VENOM?! OF ALL THE TIMES TO RUN INTO THIS NUTJOB!
WHAT'RE YOU UP TO THIS TIME, EDDIE?
THIS IS MY CALLING, LI! TO WIPE EVERY TRACE OF YOU--
--OFF THE FACE OF THE EARTH!
PERFECT. LOOKS LIKE BROCK'S TINFOIL HAT IS RECEIVING ALL KINDS OF CRAZY TODAY.
HE'S TRYING TO WHACK MARTIN LI? NEW YORK'S PATRON SAINT OF THE SOUP KITCHENS?
IF EVER THERE WAS A NEED FOR SPIDER-MAN--
--BUT AUNT MAY--?
PETER? DID I LOSE YOU?
NO, JAY. STILL HERE. I-I DON'T KNOW WHAT TO DO!

WHAT DO YOU MEAN?
THERE'S A... CAR ACCIDENT UP AHEAD.
ARE YOU ALL RIGHT?
YEAH, I'M FINE. IT'S JUST--I THINK I CAN HELP.
EMT
BUT WITH MAY ON THE WAY TO THE HOSPITAL, HOW CAN I...?
JAY, GIVE ME THAT.
PETER, LISTEN TO ME, I'M OKAY...
AUNT MAY? YOU SHOULDN'T BE--
HUSH. JAY'S HERE. HE'S MY HUSBAND AND HE'LL LOOK AFTER ME. BUT YOU...
...IF SOMEONE'S IN TROUBLE, AND YOU CAN HELP?
YOU BETTER DO EVERYTHING IN YOUR POWER TO DO SO! KNOW WHY?
WHY?
BECAUSE THAT'S HOW YOUR UNCLE BEN AND I RAISED YOU.
YES, MA'AM. OH, AND LADY, YOU ARE ONE IN A MILLION. SEE YOU SOON.
VOICE COMMAND: END CALL.
IT'S SPIDEY TIME.

HEY, CHUCKLES. THE AUTO SHOP CALLED. THE CUSTOMER LOVES THE NEW SUNROOF--
--BUT THE MONSTER-SHAPED HOOD ORNAMENT HAS GOT TO GO!
SMAKK
GYAH!
SPIDER-MAN?! THANK YOU! FOR COMING TO MY AID...
...AGAIN.
FOR YOU, MR. LI? ANYTIME!
KTAM
FOOL! DO YOU KNOW WHAT YOU'VE DONE?!

GENTLEMEN, ONCE AGAIN SPIDER-MAN HAS SEEN FIT TO INVOLVE HIMSELF IN MY PLANS.
I SHOULD BE READY FOR HIM AS WELL. HAVE THE LAB PREPARE THE LAST VIALS OF THE DEVIL'S BREATH.
YES, SIR.

YOU LET THE REAL MONSTER GET AWAY!
UNH!
WHAT?! MARTIN LI?

WOW! WHO'S NEXT ON YOUR LIST? MOTHER TERESA? THE EASTER BUNNY? RACHAEL RAY?
YOU'VE REALLY GONE ALL COO-COO FOR COCOA PUFFS, HAVEN'T YOU, BROCK?
SLSHH
SHUT UP! YOU REALLY DID IT, DIDN'T YOU?
OW!

WEB-SHOOTERS: WEB-BARRAGE! FULL SPREAD!
HAD ME THINKING YOU WERE ONE OF THE GOOD GUYS!
THWIP-IP-IP
THWIP-IP-IP
KEEP FORGETTING, SOMETHING ABOUT BROCK'S NEW POWERS...

...THEY PLAY HAVOC WITH MINE! SPIDER-SPEED'S GONE!
THE PERFECT LITTLE SUPER HERO!
WHA MP
BUT IF YOU'RE SIDING WITH MARTIN LI...
KRAK
THERE GOES THE SPIDER-STRENGTH!
TOOM
...YOU'RE ON THE WRONG SIDE!
GNHH!
AND THAT MEANS I HAVE TO TEACH YOU SOMETHING, SPIDER.
ONE FINAL LESSON.
C-CAN'T LET HIM GET HIS CLAWS INTO ME. OR HE'LL "CURE" ME.
TAKE AWAY MY POWERS FOR GOOD. HAVE TO...
...

G SPIDER
Y FRANK C

YOU AND ME, WE'VE GOT TRUST ISSUES.
I ADMIT, I TOOK IT PERSONALLY. BUT THEN I REMEMBERED YOU ALWAYS START THIS WAY WITH YOUR FRIENDS. DAREDEVIL, THE FF, THE AVENGERS...
YOU FIGHT. GET TO KNOW EACH OTHER BETTER...THEN YOU TEAM UP.
The Return Of Anti-Venom
BUT I'M PRESSED FOR TIME. SO LET'S SPEED THIS UP. YOU KNOW I'M EDDIE BROCK...
...LET'S SEE WHO YOU ARE.
BAD ENOUGH ANTI-VENOM'S A PSYCHO, HE'S GOTTA BE A CLINGY PSYCHO. AND HIS GOOP MESSES UP MY POWERS... HAS ME TOO WEAK TO BREAK FREE...
Part Two: Revelation Day

FORTUNATELY, I CAN BE CLINGY TOO.
HEY! WHAT'D YOU DO, GLUE IT ON?
STICKY SKIN. GOOD TO KNOW SOME OF MY POWERS STILL WORK.

WHAT WOULD YOU THINK OF ME IF I LET YOU TAKE MY MASK OFF ON THE FIRST DATE?
YOU ACT LIKE I'M ELECTRO OR SANDMAN. I'M ON YOUR SIDE NOW!
BUT I GET IT. I NEED TO EARN YOUR TRUST. AND I WILL.

HANG OUT IN THE LAIR WHILE I... "RUN SOME ERRANDS."
YOUR LAIR SMELLS FUNKY.
LINGERING METH FUMES. IT WAS A DRUG LAB UNTIL I SHUT IT DOWN.
SEE? THAT'S ME NOW: CRIME-FIGHTER.

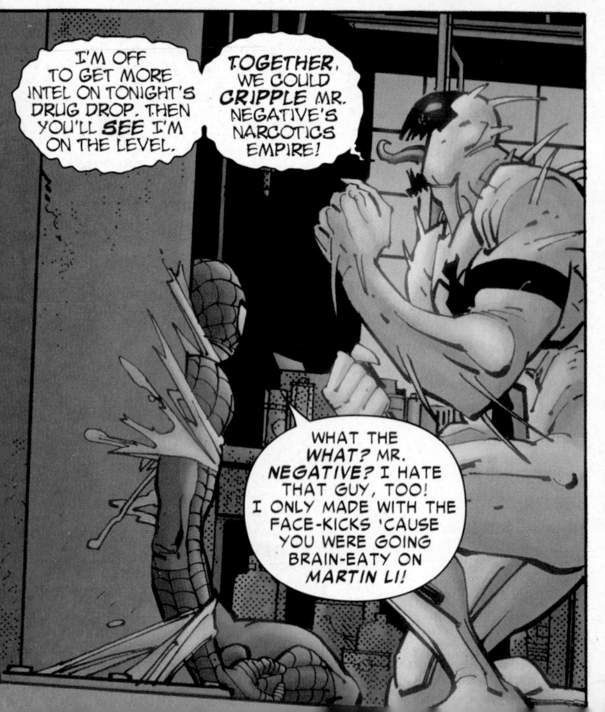
I'M OFF TO GET MORE INTEL ON TONIGHT'S DRUG DROP. THEN YOU'LL SEE I'M ON THE LEVEL.
TOGETHER, WE COULD CRIPPLE MR. NEGATIVE'S NARCOTICS EMPIRE!
WHAT THE WHAT? MR. NEGATIVE? I HATE THAT GUY, TOO! I ONLY MADE WITH THE FACE-KICKS 'CAUSE YOU WERE GOING BRAIN-EATY ON MARTIN LI!

THAT'S WHAT I'VE BEEN TRYING TO TELL YOU.
MARTIN LI IS MR. NEGATIVE.

MARTIN LI? THE GUY WHO FOUNDED THE F.E.A.S.T. PROJECT TO HELP THE HOMELESS...
...IS THE SUPER-POWERED CRIME LORD OF CHINATOWN?
EDDIE, YOU'VE BEEN INHALING TOO MANY METH FUMES. THEY DON'T EVEN LOOK ALIKE.
THAT'S HIS NEGATIVE IMAGE EFFECT, IT TRICKS YOUR EYES!

SEE, THIS IS WHAT I'M ALKING ABOUT! O ONE TAKES CRAZY EDDIE BROCK SERIOUSLY!
BUT I'LL SHOW YOU. I'LL SHOW EVERYBODY!

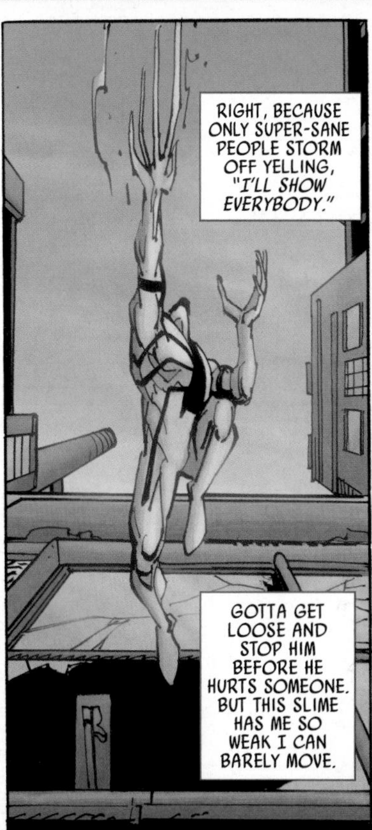
RIGHT, BECAUSE ONLY SUPER-SANE PEOPLE STORM OFF YELLING, "I'LL SHOW EVERYBODY."
GOTTA GET LOOSE AND STOP HIM BEFORE HE HURTS SOMEONE. BUT THIS SLIME HAS ME SO WEAK I CAN BARELY MOVE.

GOOD THING I ADDED SPECIAL VOICE-COMMANDS FOR MY WEB SHOOTERS. AND SINCE EDDIE DIDN'T CLEAN UP THE METH LAB...
RIGHT SHOOTER... RECOIL STRAND... FIRE!
THWIP

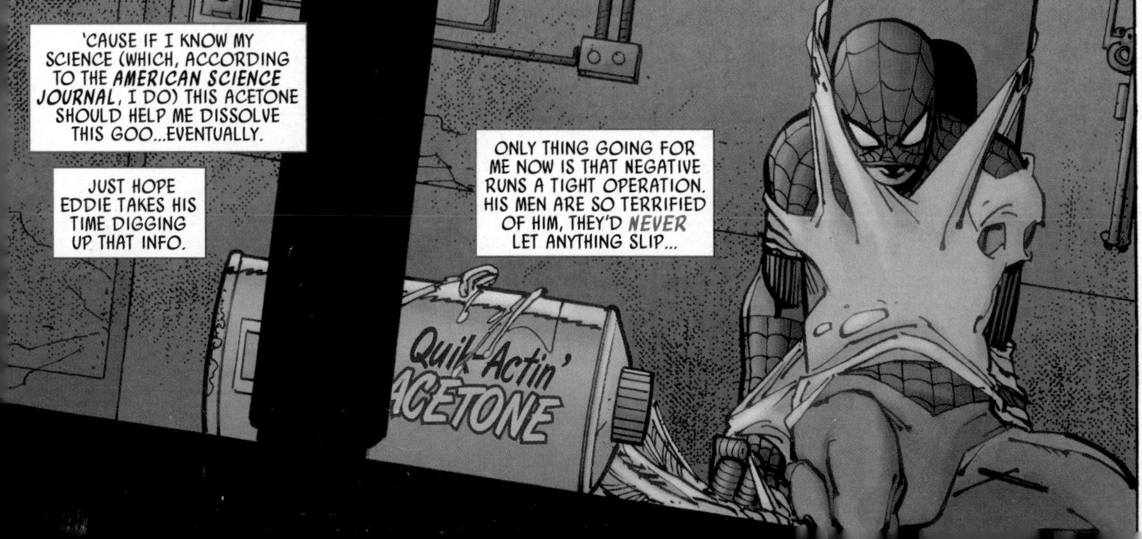
'CAUSE IF I KNOW MY SCIENCE (WHICH, ACCORDING TO THE AMERICAN SCIENCE JOURNAL, I DO) THIS ACETONE SHOULD HELP ME DISSOLVE THIS GOO...EVENTUALLY.
JUST HOPE EDDIE TAKES HIS TIME DIGGING UP THAT INFO.
ONLY THING GOING FOR ME NOW IS THAT NEGATIVE RUNS A TIGHT OPERATION. HIS MEN ARE SO TERRIFIED OF HIM, THEY'D NEVER LET ANYTHING SLIP...
Quik-Actin' ACETONE

Rothner Antiques.
IN THE WEST VILLAGE.
IF I TALK, HE'LL KILL ME! JAIL, WITNESS PROTECTION...
MR. NEGATIVE CAN GET TO ME ANYWHERE!
CAN HE REACH YOU IN THE AFTERLIFE, "BEN ROTHNER"? THAT'S WHERE YOU'LL HAVE TO ANSWER TO THE WRAITH...FOR ALL ETERNITY!
AND YOU HAVE MANY SINS TO ANSWER FOR, DON'T YOU, ROBERT ROSS? FROM THE DAYS WHEN YOU SMUGGLED NOT ART, BUT HUMAN BEINGS...PACKED INTO SHIPPING CRATES, STARVING, COLD...
OH, YES, I SEE IT ALL. CHANGING YOUR NAME DIDN'T WASH THE GUILT FROM YOUR SOUL, ROBERT.

HOW MANY DIED, SUFFERING IN THE DARK? HOW MANY LIVED ON IN AGONY, SOLD INTO SLAVERY?
H-HOW DID YOU--NO ONE ALIVE KNOWS MY REAL NAME.

NO. NO ONE ALIVE.
BUT JEAN DEWOLFF HASN'T BEEN ALIVE FOR A LONG, LONG TIME.
OH, GOD...

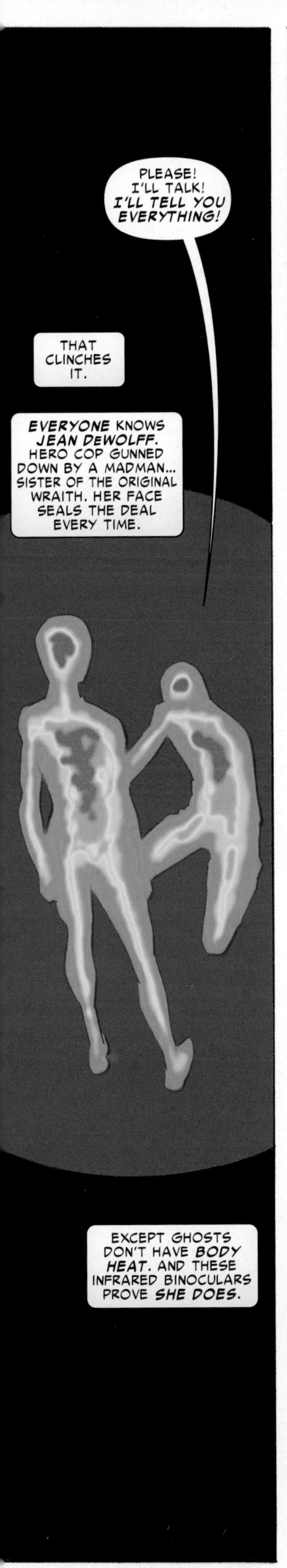
PLEASE! I'LL TALK! I'LL TELL YOU EVERYTHING!
THAT CLINCHES IT.
EVERYONE KNOWS JEAN DEWOLFF. HERO COP GUNNED DOWN BY A MADMAN... SISTER OF THE ORIGINAL WRAITH. HER FACE SEALS THE DEAL EVERY TIME.
EXCEPT GHOSTS DON'T HAVE BODY HEAT. AND THESE INFRARED BINOCULARS PROVE SHE DOES.

THE CIRCUMSTANTIAL EVIDENCE IS STRONG... BUT FACE IT, CARLIE, YOU'RE A FORENSIC SCIENTIST.
YOU NEED PROOF.
TONIGHT! MORE HEROIN THAN YOU'VE EVER SEEN...
HE'S TAKING A DELIVERY TONIGHT!

SO YOU'LL COME FACE-TO-FACE WITH THE WRAITH LATER...
...ONCE YOU'VE REMOVED ALL DOUBT ABOUT WHO SHE REALLY IS.
ROTHNERS ANTIQUES

Columbia Presbyterian Medical Center.
I CAN PAY FOR ANY TEST YOU RUN. CHECK EVERYTHING--
WE ALREADY HAVE, MR. JAMESON. YOUR WIFE IS FINE. JUST A FAINTING SPELL.
JAY, HUSH. THEY'RE TALKING ABOUT MR. LI. I WANT TO MAKE SURE HE'S ALL RIGHT AFTER BEING ATTACKED BY SOME MONSTER.

--LIVE AT THE METROPOLITAN MUSEUM AS MAYOR J. JONAH JAMESON INTRODUCES PHILANTHROPIST MARTIN LI.
SEE, MAY, HE'S FINE. I WISH YOU'D WORRY MORE ABOUT YOURSELF.

I WANT TO PERSONALLY THANK MARTIN LI FOR DONATING HIS NEWLY ACQUIRED COLLECTION OF CHINESE TERRACOTTA WARRIORS TO THE METROPOLITAN MUSEUM.
PROVING ONCE AGAIN THERE'S NO NEED TO SPEND YOUR TOURIST DOLLARS ANYWHERE BUT IN NEW YORK, BECAUSE ANYTHING IN THE WORLD WORTH SEEING ENDS UP HERE!
AHEM.
OH, YES...AND FOR AN UP CLOSE AND PERSONAL EXPERIENCE, BUY TICKETS TO ONE OF THE PRIVATE VIEWINGS...WITH ALL PROCEEDS GOING TO HELP THE HOMELESS!
UNBELIEVABLE.
REC

--AS MARTIN LI STRIKES ANOTHER BLOW AGAINST HOMELESSNESS. I'M NORAH WINTERS, AND YOU'RE WATCHING THE DAILY BUGLE, STREAMING LIVE...
...BECAUSE READING'S TOO HARD FOR SOME PEOPLE AND PRINT, APPARENTLY, IS DEAD.
AND WE'RE CLEAR.
HEY!

NORAH, WHAT IS THIS? I'M YOUR CAMERAMAN! SINCE WHEN DOES RANDY HAVE ANY TRAINING?
WELL, SINCE ANY IDIOT CAN POINT AND SHOOT, I FIGURED I'D HELP MY GIRL WITH HER WORK.

SINCE THAT'S ALL SHE SEEMS TO HAVE TIME FOR THESE DAYS.
IDIOT, RIGHT. I GUESS AN IDIOT COULD'VE GOTTEN THOSE SHOTS I BROUGHT YOU OF HOBGOBLIN FIGHTING HERCULES AND SPIDER-GIRL.*
BUT HEY, NO BIG. YOU WANT A NEW CAMERAMAN, I'M SURE I CAN FIND ANOTHER REPORTER TO WORK WITH.
SEE HERC #2 AND SPIDER-GIRL #6.

H, COME ON, PHIL, RANDY WAS JUST MESSING WITH YOU. TRUTH IS, WITH THE MAZING WORK YOU'VE BEEN DOING, I DIDN'T WANT TO BUG YOU FOR A PUFF PIECE.
BUT SINCE YOU'RE HERE, I'M GOING TO TRY AND BAG AN INTERVIEW WITH LI, IF YOU WANT TO TAG ALONG.
UHH... SURE.

AFTER ALL I'VE DONE FOR HER, SHE KEEPS GOING BACK TO HIM. AND HE'S OBVIOUSLY NOT GOING TO GIVE HER UP.
I MIGHT HAVE TO FIND A PERMANENT SOLUTION TO THE RANDY ROBERTSON PROBLEM...

...AND FOR A MEASLY ONE THOUSAND DOLLAR DONATION, YOU GET A PHOTO WITH ME!
SIR, PARDON ME, BUT WE HAVE, AH... ARRANGEMENTS TO MAKE.
IS IT POSSIBLE TO TALK... BUSINESS...?
IT'S FINE. THAT BLOWHARD JAMESON WOULD SOONER DIE THAN RELINQUISH THE SPOTLIGHT. THERE'S NO FURTHER NEED FOR MARTIN LI.
YOU ARE SPEAKING TO MR. NEGATIVE.
THE LAST OF THE WARRIORS HAVE CLEARED CUSTOMS. THI MUSEUM'S AGREED TO LET YOUR PERSONAL STAFF PREPARE THEM FOR EXHIBITION.

THEY'VE PROVIDED US CODES TO DEACTIVATE THE ALARMS IN THAT SECTION OF THE BUILDING.
OUR CLEANING CREW WILL BRING IN INDUSTRIAL STRENGTH VACUUMS, AS WELL AS THE SPECIAL SOLUTION TO DISSOLVE THE PLUGS IN THE FIGURES.
IT WILL TAKE NO MORE THAN TWO HOURS TO EXTRACT THE "PRODUCT" WITHIN AND REMOVE IT AS TRASH.

THE PERFECT CRIME, HUH, LI? AND THE PERFECT CHANCE TO CATCH YOU IN THE ACT...
...PROVING TO SPIDER-MAN I'M EVERY BIT AS SANE AS HE IS.

OW! OW! OW!
THIS WAS CRAZY! I'M JUST GONNA BURN OFF MY--
WAIT. THINK I FELT IT GIVE...

COME ON, PETE. THIS STUFF SUPPRESSES YOUR POWERS, IT DOESN'T TAKE THEM AWAY.
YOU CAN DO THIS. DIG DOWN...KEEP FIGHTING...
YAAAH!

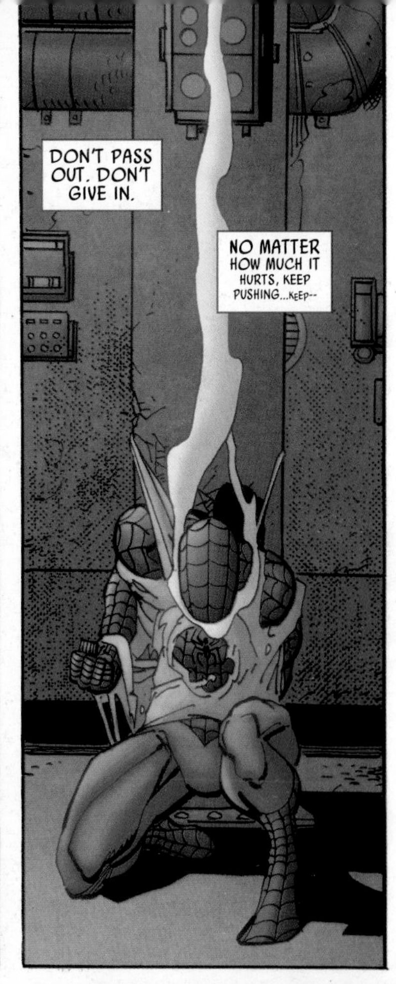
DON'T PASS OUT. DON'T GIVE IN.
NO MATTER HOW MUCH IT HURTS, KEEP PUSHING...KEEP--

YES!!

SPLORKCH
BLUHH!

HEY, PARTNER.
OH, COME ON!

I KNOW, YOU'VE BEEN BORED. BUT CHEER UP. THIS IS WHERE THE FUN STARTS.
WE'RE TAKING A FIELD TRIP...TO THE MUSEUM. YOU'LL LOVE IT.
IT'LL BE VERY EDUCATIONAL.

HALF A DAY STUCK TO A WALL AND NOW HE'S CARTING ME AROUND LIKE A SLIME-COVERED HELLO KITTY BACKPACK. THIS IS SO HUMILIATING.
I'M AN AVENGER! I'M NOT SUPPOSED TO GET JOBBED LIKE THIS!
SO, BE HONEST... DOES WOLVERINE CARRY YOU TO CRIME SCENES?
DUDE, YOU REALLY NEED A GIRLFRIEND.

Special Crimes Evidence Storage.
I WANT TO RUN SOME TESTS ON IT...SEE IF I CAN TIE IT TO AN OPEN CASE.
SORRY, CARLIE... CAN'T HELP YOU.
DON'T TELL ME. IT'S *MISSING*, RIGHT?
WE HANDLE *DANGEROUS EQUIPMENT* USED BY *SUPERHUMAN CRIMINALS*. WE DON'T *LET* EVIDENCE GO "*MISSING*."

IT WAS *DESTROYED*. THERE WAS AN ACCIDENT...AN OLD PUMPKIN BOMB WENT OFF. LUCKY NOBODY GOT *KILLED*.
REALLY? WOW. CAN I SEE THE REPORT?

BINGO. THE "*DESTROYED*" EVIDENCE INCLUDED CANISTERS OF MR. FEAR'S GAS, A BUNCH OF MYSTERIO'S TECH...
...PLUS THE *MASK* MYSTERIO WAS GOING TO USE TO MAKE IT LOOK LIKE *JEAN DeWOLFF* WAS BACK FROM THE DEAD.
AS SEEN WAAY BACK IN ASM #620!--SW

AND BIG SURPRISE: THE ONLY PERSON IN THE EVIDENCE ROOM AT THE TIME OF THE "*ACCIDENT*"...
...WAS CAPTAIN YURI WATANABE.

FIND OUT ANYTHING USEFUL, KID?
SURE DID, CLIFF. QUESTION NOW IS...
...WHAT DO I DO WITH IT?

The Metropolitan Museum of Art.
YOU'RE LEAVING ME GOOPED UP TO A NAKED GUY'S BUTT? NOW YOU'RE JUST BEING MEAN.
NOBODY'LL FIND YOU HERE. AFTER I TAKE DOWN NEGATIVE, I'LL BRING HIM IN. SHOW YOU I'M RIGHT.
SERIOUSLY, EDDIE, IF MR. NEGATIVE'S AROUND, YOU'RE GONNA NEED HELP.
NO. HE MIGHT BE HERE AS MARTIN LI, AND THE LAST TIME YOU SAW ME...TRYING TO APPREHEND HIM, YOU LOST IT.
YOU WERE TRYING TO TEAR OFF HIS HEAD!
DETAILS.
DARK. LOOKS LIKE I BEAT 'EM HERE.
GUESS I'LL SET UP AN AMBUSH...SOMEWHERE I CAN JUMP OUT AND REALLY DO SOME--

SHHKK
RRAAAAGGH!

SMOOTH. I'LL GIVE YOU THAT.
BUT I HEAL SHOTGUN WOUNDS IN **SECONDS**. YOU THINK SOME PIG-STICKER IS GONNA STOP--

--STOP...
OH, DEAR. IT APPEARS SOMETHING'S HAPPENED TO YOUR HEALING ABILITY.
SOMETHING... ***NEGATIVE.***
I KNOW WHO YOU ARE, EDDIE BROCK. AND WHATEVER GIFT MARTIN LI UNWITTINGLY GAVE YOU, I CAN TAKE AWAY.

GNNH! C'MON!
WHAT I WOULDN'T GIVE FOR SOME ACETONE RIGHT ABOUT--
SPIDER-MAN...
UM...NO SPIDER-MEN HERE. JUST US STATUES.
YOU'VE NOTHING TO FEAR. WE WERE ALLIES WHEN I LIVED. WE CAN BE ALLIES AGAIN.

I AM THE WRAITH. I KNOW YOU HAVE QUESTIONS. THERE'S NO TIME. WE HAVE TO--
OH. I DON'T HAVE QUESTIONS. I'VE MET SPIRITS OF VENGEANCE, LADY, AND YOU AIN'T ONE OF 'EM.
SLSHH
SLSHH
I RECOGNIZE ALL THAT TECH. MYSTERIO'S, RIGHT?

BUT IF YOU'RE HERE TO STOP BAD GUYS, COUNT ME IN.
RIGHT NOW, MY STANDARDS FOR PARTNERS ARE PRETTY LOW.
...

LET'S GO.

SPIDER-MAN WAS RIGHT. I AM CRAZY.

TAKING ON NEGATIVE ALONE... LEAVING THE GUY WHO COULD HELP ME TIED UP. AND NOW I'M GONNA BE CRAZY AND DEAD...
FAREWELL, EDWARD.
HEY. PARTNER!

QUIT HOGGING ALL THE ACTION!
KRAK
THOK
WHAT--?

DEAL WITH THE WOMAN!
I'LL FINISH SPIDER-MAN MYSELF!

SPIDER-MAN! MY FEAR GAS ISN'T AFFECTING THEM!
YEAH, I WAS AFRAID OF THAT.

I THINK THEY GET THEIR POWERS FROM NEGATIVE.

IF I CAN TAKE *HIM* OUT--

--GUHH!
IF WISHES WERE HORSES, BEGGARS WOULD RIDE.

HEY.
IMPOSSIBLE!

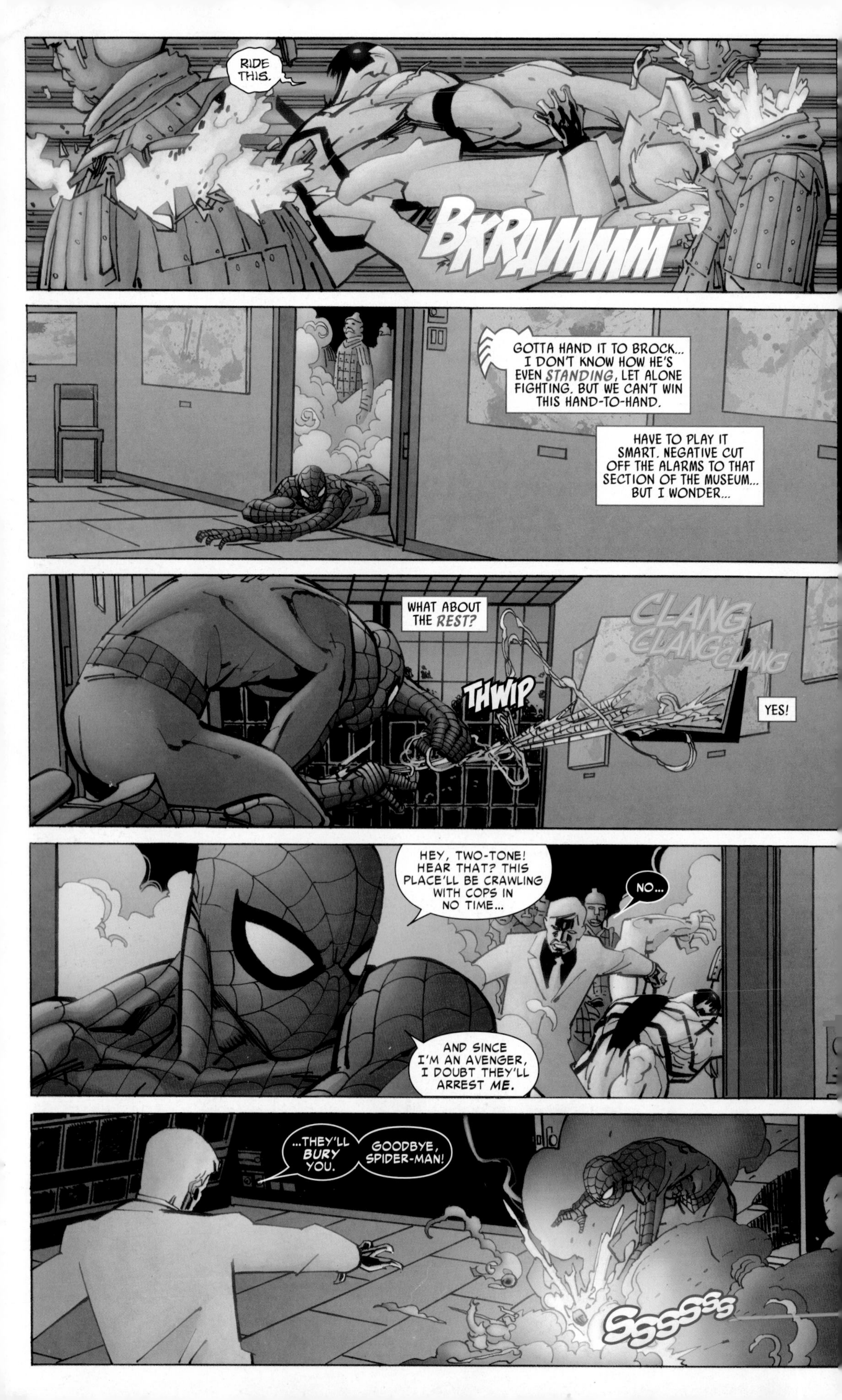
RIDE THIS.
BKRAMMM
GOTTA HAND IT TO BROCK... I DON'T KNOW HOW HE'S EVEN STANDING, LET ALONE FIGHTING. BUT WE CAN'T WIN THIS HAND-TO-HAND.
HAVE TO PLAY IT SMART. NEGATIVE CUT OFF THE ALARMS TO THAT SECTION OF THE MUSEUM... BUT I WONDER...
WHAT ABOUT THE REST?
THWIP
CLANG CLANG CLANG
YES!
HEY, TWO-TONE! HEAR THAT? THIS PLACE'LL BE CRAWLING WITH COPS IN NO TIME...
NO...
AND SINCE I'M AN AVENGER, I DOUBT THEY'LL ARREST ME.
...THEY'LL BURY YOU.
GOODBYE, SPIDER-MAN!
SSSSSS

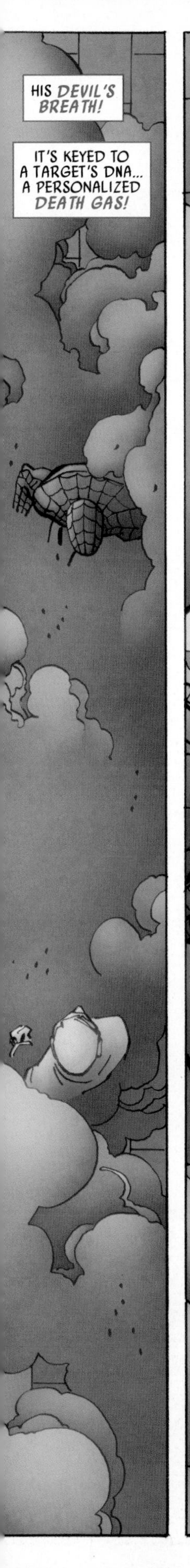
HIS DEVIL'S BREATH!
IT'S KEYED TO A TARGET'S DNA... A PERSONALIZED DEATH GAS!

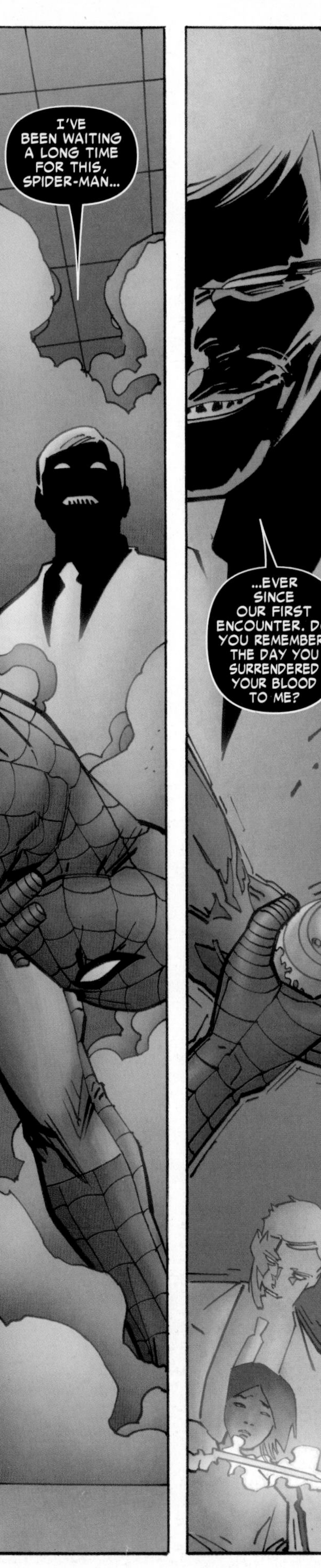
I'VE BEEN WAITING A LONG TIME FOR THIS, SPIDER-MAN...
...EVER SINCE OUR FIRST ENCOUNTER. DO YOU REMEMBER THE DAY YOU SURRENDERED YOUR BLOOD TO ME?

YEAH. JUST LIKE YESTERDAY. KNOW WHAT ELSE I REMEMBER?
THE TIME BLACK CAT AND I SWAPPED THAT BLOOD FOR PIG'S BLOOD, RIGHT UNDER YOUR NEGATIVE NOSE.

SEE, I'VE BEEN WAITING A LONG TIME FOR THIS, TOO. LAST TIME WE TUSSLED, YOU HIT ME WITH A SHOT THAT'D MAKE THE HULK PROUD.
BUT NOW? WITH YOUR DEFENSES DOWN? LORDING THIS OVER ME? THIS IS IT. RIGHT HERE. MY ONE CHANCE. EVERYTHING I'VE GOT IN ONE PUNCH--ALL OR NOTHING...

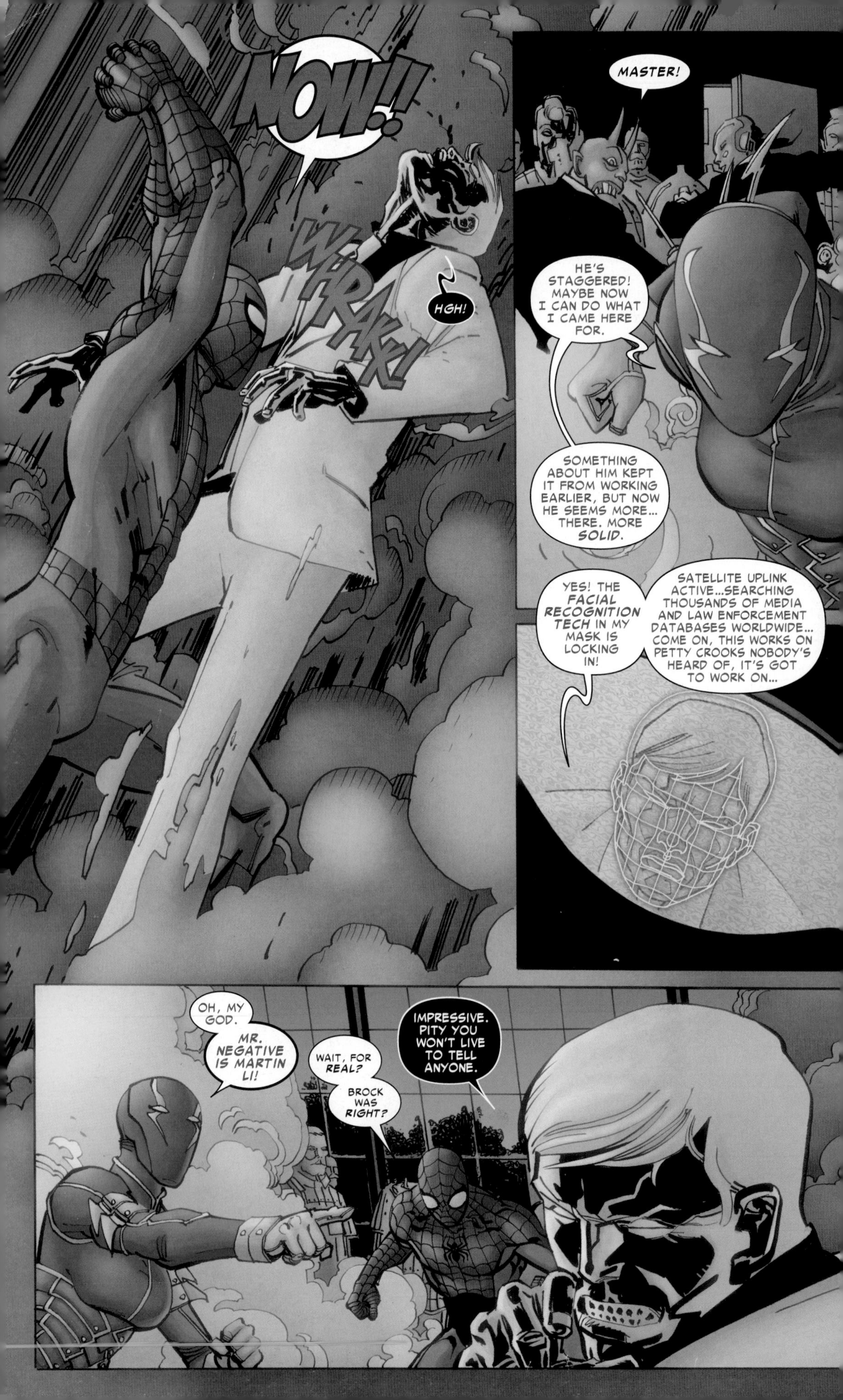
NOW!!
WHAK!
HGH!
MASTER!
HE'S STAGGERED! MAYBE NOW I CAN DO WHAT I CAME HERE FOR.
SOMETHING ABOUT HIM KEPT IT FROM WORKING EARLIER, BUT NOW HE SEEMS MORE... THERE. MORE SOLID.
YES! THE FACIAL RECOGNITION TECH IN MY MASK IS LOCKING IN!
SATELLITE UPLINK ACTIVE...SEARCHING THOUSANDS OF MEDIA AND LAW ENFORCEMENT DATABASES WORLDWIDE... COME ON, THIS WORKS ON PETTY CROOKS NOBODY'S HEARD OF, IT'S GOT TO WORK ON...
OH, MY GOD.
MR. NEGATIVE IS MARTIN LI!
WAIT, FOR REAL?
BROCK WAS RIGHT?
IMPRESSIVE. PITY YOU WON'T LIVE TO TELL ANYONE.

OH, BUT I DID.
I JUST TOLD EVERYONE.

The Daily Bugle.
EVERY COMPUTER, TV AND SMART PHONE IN RANGE IS SEEING WHAT I SEE.
THIS IS EXACTLY WHAT HAPPENED TO OSBORN LAST YEAR. ALL OVER AGAIN.
SCOOPED ON ANOTHER SPIDER-MAN STORY. WE'RE SLIPPING, PEOPLE.

Gracie Mansion.
MR. NEGATIVE'S FACE SIDE-BY-SIDE WITH MARTIN LI'S, WITH A NINETY-FIVE PERCENT NODAL POINT MATCH...
ON THE SAME DAY I DO A PHOTO OP WITH THE MAN! HOW COULD HE DO THIS-- TO ME?!
NO REASON TO BLAME YOURSELF, MR. MAYOR.
OF COURSE NOT! I BLAME SPIDER-MAN!

Residence of the Jamesons.
...PLUS A POSITIVE SKINPRINT MATCH, WHICH CAN DISTINGUISH BETWEEN IDENTICAL TWINS.
MAY...YOU BETTER SIT DOWN.
NONSENSE, JAY, THE DOCTOR SAID THERE WAS NOTHING TO WORRY ABOUT...

...MARTIN?
NO. IT CAN'T BE...

OOH-OOH.
I'M THINKING MR. NEGATIVE'S MOOD IS ABOUT TO MATCH HIS NAME.

YOU... DARE?
DO YOU HAVE ANY IDEA WHAT YOU'VE RUINED? HOW LONG IT TOOK ME TO BUILD--?
MASTER, WE MUST GO! THE POLICE--
WEEOOWEEOOWEEOO

AN ALMOND SMELL...THAT'S CYANIDE! STAY BACK!
HE'S NOT KIDDING AROUND. FORGET DEVIL'S BREATH--THAT'D KILL ANYONE!
THERE WILL BE TIME FOR VENGEANCE LATER.
AND IT WILL BE TERRIBLE.

EVEN THE "GHOST OF JEAN DEWOLFF."
WRAITH.
I'M FINE, BUT I HAVE TO GO... I CAN'T FACE THE POLICE.

EVERYONE RUNS WHILE I WAIT FOR THE COPS. SUDDENLY I'M THE GROWN-UP.
AND WHAT DID I TELL YOU ABOUT RUNNING WITH SAMURAI SWORDS?

SERIOUSLY, ARE YOU OKAY? I'VE SEEN YOU HEAL FROM BULLET WOUNDS IN, LIKE, TWO SECONDS...
HRRAAAA!
EDDIE? COME ON, MAN--

I'M FINE... NOW. THANKS TO YOU.
ABOUT LEAVING YOU TIED UP...MY BAD.
UH-HUH. WELL, AS LONG AS WE'RE SAYING OUR SORRIES AND ALL...

WHAT CAN I SAY? MUCH AS I HATE TO ADMIT IT...
(AND THAT'S ABOUT AS MUCH AS I WANT TO PUNCH YOU REPEATEDLY IN THE FACE)
YOU WERE RIGHT.

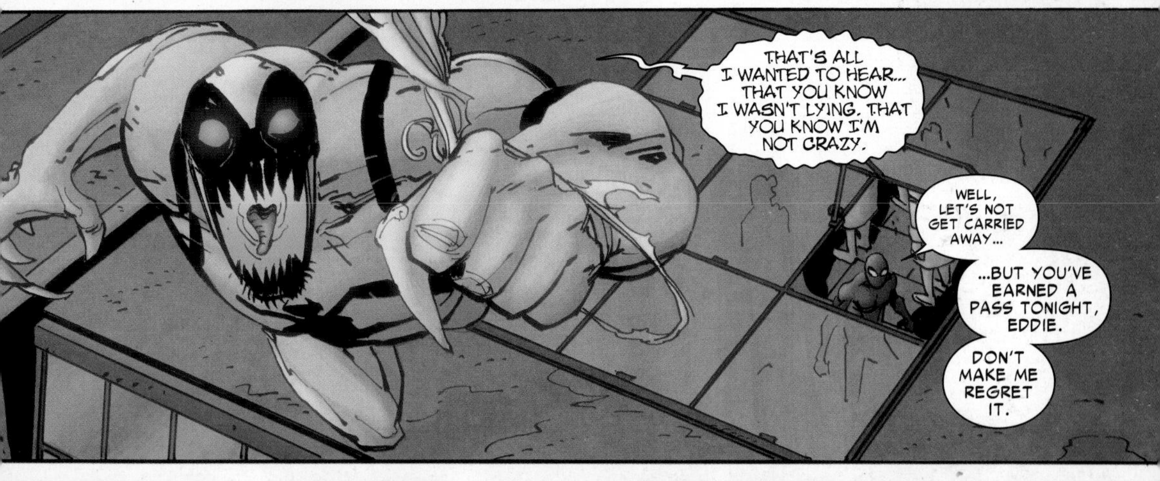
THAT'S ALL I WANTED TO HEAR... THAT YOU KNOW I WASN'T LYING. THAT YOU KNOW I'M NOT CRAZY.
WELL, LET'S NOT GET CARRIED AWAY...
...BUT YOU'VE EARNED A PASS TONIGHT, EDDIE.
DON'T MAKE ME REGRET IT.

POLICE! NOBODY MOVE!
IT'S OKAY, OFFICERS. I'LL EXPLAIN EVERYTHING--

--AS SOON AS I TAKE A BATHROOM BREAK.
THOSE STATUES ARE FULL OF HEROIN. DISCUSS.
BE RIGHT BACK.
CARLIE? BUT WHERE'S SHE GOING?

OH--CARLIE. I HEARD THE CALL ON MY RADIO--I WAS JUST--
CAPTAIN WATANABE... STOP.
I KNOW.
NYPD

I KNOW YOU'RE THE WRAITH.
HOW DID YOU--?

"MY PHONE. I SLIPPED IT INTO YOUR POCKET EARLIER AND FOLLOWED THE G.P.S.--"

OF COURSE YOU FOUND OUT, IT WAS ONLY A MATTER OF TIME.
YOU'RE GOOD, COOPER.

I KNOW HOW YOU DID IT, YURI. I JUST WANT TO KNOW WHY.
YOU, OF ALL PEOPLE... WHY GO AROUND THE LAW? WHY IMPERSONATE A DEAD OFFICER AND A FRIEND?

JEAN AND I WERE CLOSE. WHEN WE LOST HER, IT WAS PEOPLE *OUTSIDE* THE SYSTEM--DAREDEVIL AND SPIDER-MAN--WHO BROUGHT DOWN THE SIN-EATER.
THEY GOT JUSTICE FOR JEAN WHEN NO ONE ELSE COULD. I NEVER FORGOT THAT.

THE WAY THINGS HAVE BEEN LATELY... PSYCHOPATHS LIKE *MASSACRE*, AND THE DEPARTMENT ESCALATING IN RESPONSE...
...I DECIDED I HAD TO DO SOMETHING. STEM THE TIDE OF DEATH WITH A DOSE OF FEAR. SCARE PEOPLE STRAIGHT...
...AND IT WORKED. UNTIL TODAY.

SO, WHAT NOW, COOPER? I KNOW YOU TURNED IN OTHER COPS. YOUR FRIEND, GONZALES--EVEN YOUR OWN *FATHER...*
YOU SHOULD KNOW, IF YOU DO THAT TO ME, IT'S NOT JUST MY *CAREER* THAT'S OVER. MR. NEGATIVE WOULD HAVE ME DEAD WITHIN A WEEK--
CAPTAIN...

I'M NOT TURNING YOU IN.
I JUST WANTED YOU TO KNOW I FIGURED IT OUT...AND OTHERS COULD, TOO. YOU HAVE TO COVER YOUR TRACKS BETTER. WE SHOULD TALK ABOUT HOW...LATER.
BUT FOR NOW, MAYBE IT'S BEST IF YOU--AND THE WRAITH--*DISAPPEAR* FOR A WHILE.

UNDERSTOOD. AND THANK YOU, OFFICER COOPER.
THAT'LL BE ALL FOR NOW.
YES, MA'AM.

FINALLY...AT LONG LAST...THEY KNOW I WAS RIGHT. EVERYONE KNOWS.
THIS IS THE DAY EVERYTHING CHANGES.
THE DAY IT ALL TURNS AROUND...
THE DAY I'M THE HERO.
NTRAL
AL
Chinatown.
UHH... WH-WHERE--
CLINK
CHAINS? OH, GOD...
HELLO? THIS IS MARTIN LI! LOOK, WHATEVER YOU WANT, I CAN PAY IT!
PLEASE, I'LL GIVE YOU ANYTHING! JUST LET ME OUT! PLEASE!
WE MUST OBEY! HE IS STILL OUR MASTER!
NO. THAT IS NOT OUR MASTER.
UNTIL HE CHANGES BACK...
...HE IS NOTHING.

Across Town...
PETER PARKER'S APARTMENT.
SPIDER-MAN TOLD YOU WHAT HAPPENED TONIGHT?
UH, YEAH. HE OVERHEARD YOU. AND THERE'S SOMETHING I HAVE TO KNOW.
WHY DIDN'T YOU TURN THE CAPTAIN IN?

HELLO? BECAUSE SHE'S ONE OF THE GOOD GUYS!
I CAN KEEP A SECRET, PETER. AND SO CAN YOU, APPARENTLY. BUT THAT'S OVER...
IT'S TIME. TELL ME THE TRUTH ABOUT YOU AND SPIDER-MAN.

WHAT'S YOUR CONNECTION? WHATEVER IT IS, YOU CAN TRUST ME WITH IT.
I KNOW. AND I...
CARLIE, YOU DESERVE TO KNOW. THE TRUTH...
...THE TRUTH IS...

I--I DESIGN HIS TECH.
HIS WEB-SHOOTERS... ALL OF IT.
I KNEW IT! IT MAKES PERFECT SENSE. YOU'RE LIKE Q, IN JAMES BOND.
EXCEPT YOU'RE THE SEXY ONE.

SEE? ISN'T THAT BETTER?
KNOWING YOU'VE GOT SOMEONE YOU CAN TRUST INSTEAD OF HAVING THIS HUGE SECRET BETWEEN US?
YEAH. OF COURSE. THAT...
...THAT'S HOW IT SHOULD BE, RIGHT?
The End

AMAZING SPIDER-MAN #665
COVER BY PAOLO RIVERA

CROSSROADS

DAN SLOTT
WRITER

RYAN STEGMAN
PENCILS

MICHAEL BABINSKI
INKS

JOHN RAUCH
COLORS

VC'S JOE CARAMAGNA
LETTERS

ELLIE PYLE
ASSISTANT EDITOR

STEPHEN WACKER
SENIOR EDITOR

TOM BREVOORT
EXECUTIVE EDITOR

AXEL ALONSO
EDITOR IN CHIEF

JOE QUESADA
CHIEF CREATIVE OFFICER

DAN BUCKLEY
PUBLISHER

ALAN FINE
EXECUTIVE PRODUCER

FROM THE MOMENT I FIRST SAW HER AT THE DAILY BUGLE, *BETTY BRANT* WAS MY BIGGEST CRUSH.

BUT SHE'S SO MUCH MORE TO ME NOW: A BEST FRIEND, THE BIG SISTER I NEVER HAD, AND MY VERY OWN *"GIRL FRIDAY."*

YOU'RE A NEWSPAPER-MAN!

THAT'S WHY I'M QUITTING. I WANNA GO SOME-PLACE WHERE I CAN BE A WOMAN.

AND LATELY, THERE'S BEEN A LOT OF "STUFF."
SORRY, BETTS. I KNOW YOU WANNA SEE... WHAT WAS IT AGAIN?
CROSSROADS D'L'AMOUR.
RIGHT. BUT I JUST GOT A CALL FROM MY BOSS. I'M GOING OUTTA TOWN...

"...WAYYY OUTTA TOWN."
WAIT! WE BLEW UP THEI STARSHIP AND IT MADE A SOUND...
...IN SPACE?!

PETER, C'MON! CROSSROADS D'L'AMOUR'S A LIMITED ENGAGEMENT.
NOT MY FAULT, BETTY...

...GUYS AT WORK KINDA KIDNAPPED ME FOR THIS...THING. THAT? WE'RE PLAYING SKEE-BALL.
YEAH. AT A PLACE. KINDA LIKE A DAVE & BUSTER'S.
GOTTA GO.

BUT IT'S OKAY IF YOU WANT TO TAG ALONG, BETTY. WE'RE GOING TO THAT FILM YOU WANTED TO SEE.
NAH. GO ON YOUR DATE, GLORY. IT'S OKAY.
I'M SAVING THIS FOR PETE. AND HE PROMISED HE'D COME THROUGH FOR ME THIS TIME...

"...NO EXCUSES."
MY EMPLOYER, MR. NEGATIVE, HAS A MESSAGE FOR YOU, SPIDER-MAN.

YES. MOST WARP ENGINES CREATE MICRO ENVIRONMENTS THAT ALLOW SOUND TO TRAVEL IN--
HEY, EGGHEADS! LESS TALKIN', MORE **SKRULL-PUNCHIN'!** GOT IT?!

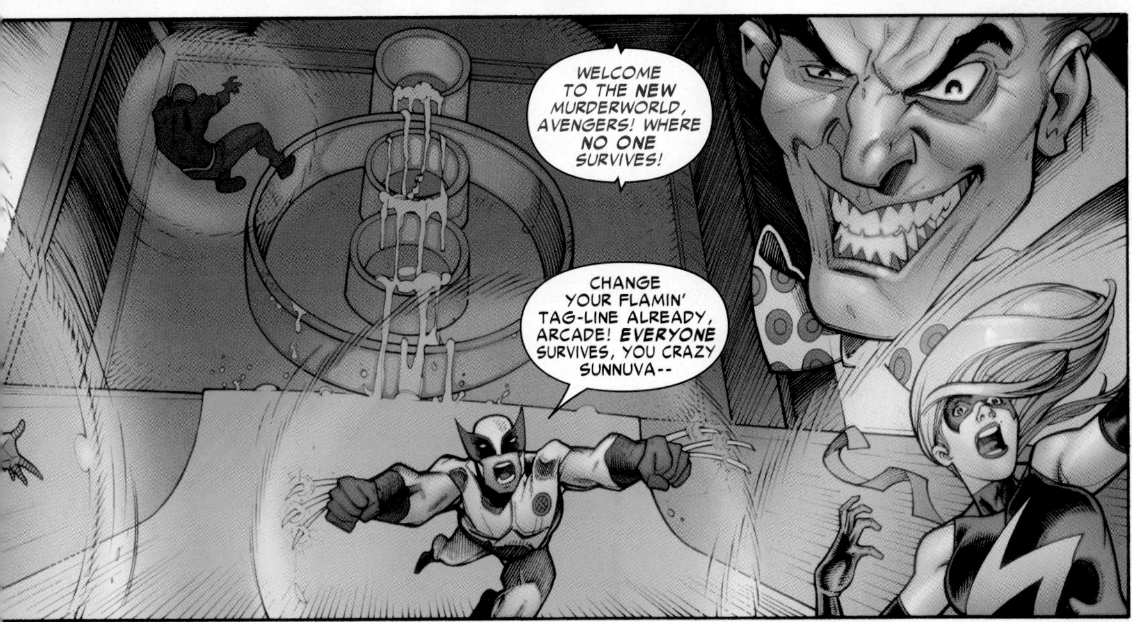
*WELCOME TO THE **NEW** MURDERWORLD, AVENGERS! WHERE **NO ONE** SURVIVES!*
CHANGE YOUR FLAMIN' TAG-LINE ALREADY, ARCADE! **EVERYONE** SURVIVES, YOU CRAZY SUNNUVA--

KTAM
GNH!
COULD YOU REPEAT IT? THINK I MISSED THE PART IN THE MIDDLE.

OW. "HAMMERHEAD"? HE OUGHTA CHANGE HIS NAME TO "HAMMERFIST." MAN, I AM STILL FEELING THAT.
PETER? ARE YOU EVEN LISTENING?
WHAT, BETTS? SORRY, LITTLE BUSY HERE AT THE MOMENT. Y'KNOW, IT'S MY--
--WORK. I KNOW.

THAT'S ALL IT EVER IS WITH YOU NOWADAYS.
EVER SINCE YOU GOT HIRED BY HORIZON LABS, IT'S ALWAYS WORK, WORK, WORK.
WELL, THAT AND BEING ON TWO AVENGERS TEAMS, THE FF, AND NIGHTLY PATROLS AS SPIDER-MAN...
NOT THAT I CAN TELL YOU THAT.
HEY, I'M AT A CRITICAL JUNCTURE HERE.
ON THE VERGE OF DISCOVERING A NEW FORM OF HYPERKINETIC ENERGY THAT COULD--

CHANGE LIFE ON EARTH AS WE KNOW IT. BLAH BLAH BLAH, Y'KNOW, MOVIE NIGHT WAS A LOT EASIER...
...BACK WHEN YOU WERE PLAIN OL' PETER PARKER, STRUGGLING FREELANCE PHOTOGRAPHER.
STOP. HOLD THE PHONE.

FOR YEARS, YOU'VE BEEN ON MY CASE TO "MAKE SOMETHING OF MYSELF." TO LIVE UP TO MY "TRUE POTENTIAL." YEARS!
AND NOW THAT I'M FINALLY DOING THAT, YOU WANT ME TO BLOW IT OFF FOR SOME STUPID MOVIE?
BUT IT'S THE LAST WEEK IT'S PLAYING--
WHATEVER. WE'LL CATCH IT ON CABLE! NOW IF YOU'LL EXCUSE ME, MS. BRANT...
...I'VE GOT THINGS TO DO!

OF ALL THE--
WHAT'S THE MATTER, BABE? YOUR "BOYFRIEND," PUNY PARKER, STAND YOU UP AGAIN?
...
YES. HMPH. I'M DONE SAVING THIS FOR HIM. LOOK, FLASH, I KNOW IT'S A FOREIGN MOVIE WITH A ZILLION SUBTITLES AND NO EXPLOSIONS...
...BUT MAYBE MY REAL BOYFRIEND COULD...?
NO CAN DO, BETTS...

"...YOU KNOW THE V.A. IS SENDING ME OFF TO A *CONFERENCE* IN WASHINGTON."
SORRY, SWEETIE...
SO LISTEN, WHEN I GET BACK, CHICK-FLICK OR NO, *I'LL* TAKE YOU.
AND THAT'S A FLASH-MAN GUARANTEE.
Orbit
NYC TAXI

...BUT IT'LL BE GONE BY THEN. IT'S ONLY PLAYING IN *ONE* THEATER IN THE CITY AS IT IS.
WHICH ONE?
THE IMPERIAL. DOWN IN *"LITTLE CHECHNYA."*

HA! BETTY, YOU'RE CRAZY. THAT'S ONE OF THE WORST SECTIONS IN TOWN!
I'VE BEEN IN SAFER HOTSPOTS IN IRAQ!
TELL YOU WHAT, LADY. IF BY SOME MIRACLE IT'S STILL PLAYING, YOUR BIG, STRONG SOLDIER-BOY WILL GET YOU THERE. DEAL?

C'MERE, YOU.

BE BACK SOON! YOU GONNA BE FINE ON YOUR OWN?
DON'T WORRY, CORPORAL THOMPSON...

...I'M BETTY BRANT. AND YOU KNOW WHAT? I'M A BIG GIRL.
AND I *AM* FINE ON MY OWN.

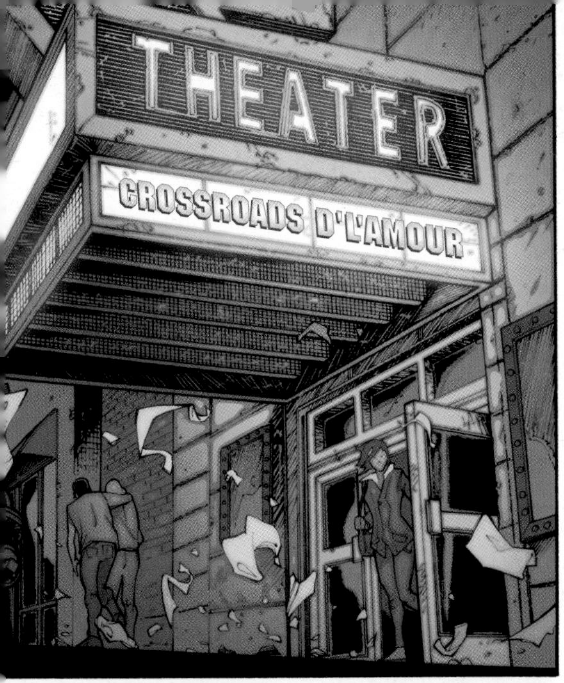
THEATER
CROSSROADS D'L'AMOUR

THEATER
CROSSROADS D'L'AMOUR
Subway
OLIVER

HEY! WHAT ARE YOU--

MMPH

Subway
THEATER
CROSSROADS D'L'AMOUR

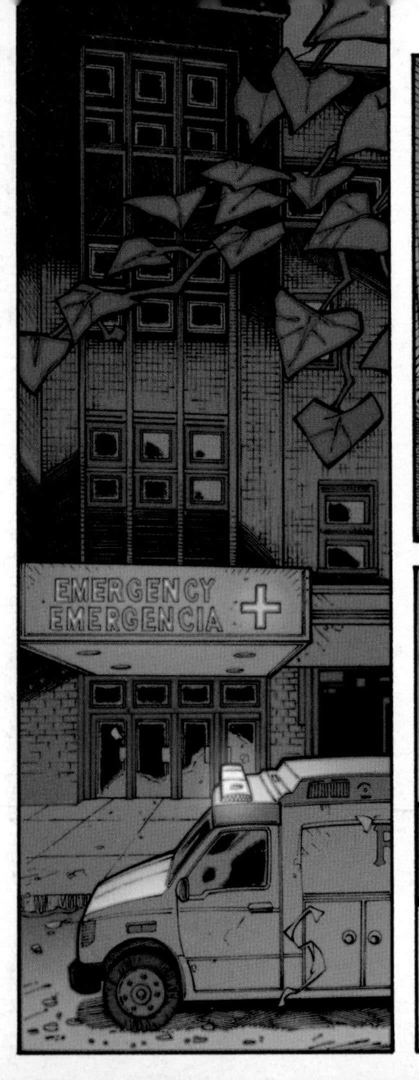
EMERGENCY
EMERGENCIA

EMERGENCY
EMERGENCIA
SOMEBODY, *HELP ME!* A DOCTOR?! ANYONE! *PLEASE!*
I'M HERE FOR *BETTY BRANT!*

I'M HER EMERGENCY CONTACT, GLORY! HER ROOMMATE. *WHERE* IS SHE?!
WHAT'S HAPPENED?!
I'M SORRY. IT DOESN'T LOOK GOOD.

HEY, THIS IS PETE. WHAT CAN I DO FOR-- WHAT?
GLORY? SLOW DOWN. WHAT'S GOING ON?
BETTY'S WHAT?! HOW DID IT..?

WHERE, GLORY? *WHERE* DID IT HAPPEN?

I KNOW THE PLACE. IT WAS WHERE WE WERE GOING TO...
RIGHT. OUR MOVIE NIGHT.
PETER PARKER: ACCESS GRANTED.

I HEAR YOU, GLORY. I UNDERSTAND. DON'T WORRY. NO...
...I'M NOT GOING TO BEAT MYSELF UP OVER IT.

STOP! THIEF! STOP HIM! IF HE MAKES IT TO THE ELEVATOR, HE'LL GET AWAY!

I OUGHTA RUN YOU IN--
SAVE YOUR BREATH, BUDDY. I'VE GOT THINGS TO DO.

I'LL BE THERE AS SOON AS I CAN. I SWEAR.
IT'S JUST FIRST...

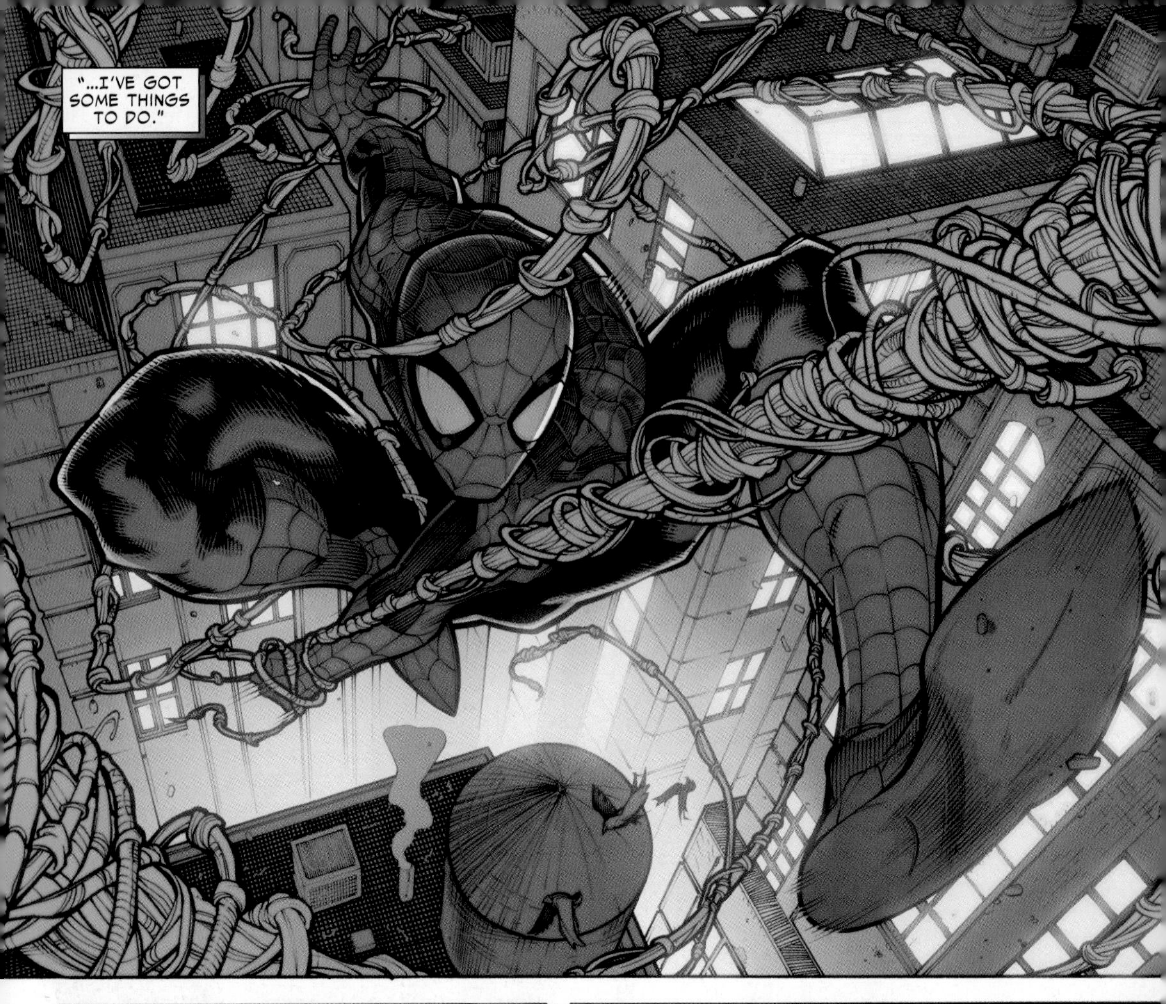
"...I'VE GOT SOME THINGS TO DO."

THIS IS REALLY INFORMATION FOR A FAMILY MEMBER, MR. ROBERTSON.
DOCTOR, WHEN IT COMES TO BETTY, WE *ARE* FAMILY. OUT WITH IT.
I WON'T LIE TO YOU. HER CONDITION'S CRITICAL. SHE SUFFERED SERIOUS HEAD TRAUMA. THERE'S SWELLING ON HER BRAIN...
...ALONG WITH A CRACKED RIB AND SOME BRUISING. IF THERE'S ANY POSITIVE NEWS, THERE'S NO SIGN OF SEXUAL ASSAULT.
EMERGENCY
WONDERFUL. I'M DOING BACKFLIPS. LIKE THAT MAKES EVERYTHING SO MUCH--
FLASH. HAS ANYONE BEEN ABLE TO REACH HIM?

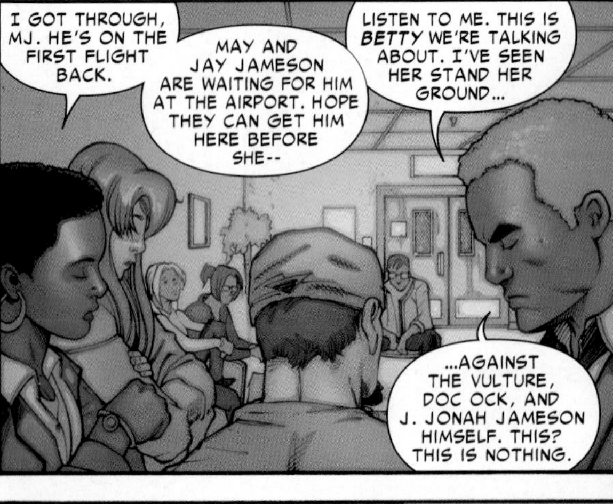
I GOT THROUGH, MJ. HE'S ON THE FIRST FLIGHT BACK.
MAY AND JAY JAMESON ARE WAITING FOR HIM AT THE AIRPORT. HOPE THEY CAN GET HIM HERE BEFORE SHE--
LISTEN TO ME. THIS IS *BETTY* WE'RE TALKING ABOUT. I'VE SEEN HER STAND HER GROUND...
...AGAINST THE VULTURE, DOC OCK, AND J. JONAH JAMESON HIMSELF. THIS? THIS IS NOTHING.

OKAY, I UNDERSTAND WHY *WE'RE* HERE. BUT WHAT ABOUT YOU, COOPER?
THIS WAS A CRIME. YOU'RE A *COP*. SHOULDN'T YOU BE OUT THERE SOLVING IT OR SOMETHING?
I'M NOT THE *ONLY* FORENSIC SCIENTIST IN NEW YORK, NORAH. AND RIGHT NOW IT'S MORE IMPORTANT I'M HERE FOR--
MS. BRANT?!

I WANT AN UPDATE ON HER STATUS RIGHT NOW!
AND EVERY TEN MINUTES TILL SHE'S BACK ON HER FEET!
OR YOU'RE *FIRED!* YOU'RE *ALL FIRED!*

SIR, I'M THE ATTENDING PHYSICIAN HERE. YOU CAN'T JUST--
I AM J. JONAH JAMESON, THE MAYOR OF NEW YORK! IN THIS CITY--
--I CAN DO WHATEVER I DAMN WELL PLEASE! NOW OUT WITH IT! HOW IS SHE?!
I WAS SAYING, THE OUTLOOK'S NOT GOOD--
ENOUGH! THIS MAN'S A QUACK!

FITZWATER! YOU'RE IN CHARGE! HAD 'IM RUSHED OVER FROM MOUNT SINAI ON MY DIME!
BEST NEUROSURGEON IN THE COUNTRY! WHEN IT COMES TO MS. BRANT, *NO* COST IS TOO GREAT!
JONAH, CALM DOWN.

ROBERTSON, DON'T YOU TELL ME TO--
PLEASE, JONAH. PEOPLE ARE ON EDGE ENOUGH.
WE KNOW YOU CARE. AND WE'RE GLAD YOU BROUGHT IN YOUR SPECIALIST, BUT TELL ME...
...WHAT'S REALLY GOING ON HERE?

I WON'T STAND FOR THIS, JOE. FIRST MARLA, AND NOW--
BETTY'S LIKE A DAUGHTER TO ME. AND THIS HAPPENED IN *MY CITY.*
I SWEAR, IF THEY THOUGHT I WAS TOUGH ON CRIME *BEFORE...*

"...AFTER WHAT THEY'VE DONE, I WILL COME DOWN ON EVERY BOTTOM-FEEDING SCUMBAG OUT THERE--
"--LIKE THE WRATH OF GOD, HIMSELF!"
KRANG
CRSHH
KRAK
YOU THINK YOU'RE CLOSED FOR TONIGHT, DIMITRI? THINK AGAIN!

RUNCH
YOU'RE CLOSED FOREVER!
YOU'VE BEEN FENCING STOLEN GOODS ON THIS BLOCK FOR TOO LONG! THAT STOPS RIGHT NOW!
AHH!

YOU AIN'T GOT NO RIGHT TO DO THIS, WALL-CRAWLER!
JUST TRYIN' TO RUN A BUSINESS HERE! THAT'S ALL!
CH-CHKK
STAY BACK!

NO!
FOR YEARS I HAVEN'T BOTHERED WITH YOU. YOU WERE SMALL-TIME.
A MIDDLEMAN, BUYING STOLEN PROPERTY. ONE STEP REMOVED.
THERE WAS NO BLOOD ON YOUR HANDS, RIGHT?

WRONG!
YOU'RE A LINK IN ONE VERY NASTY CHAIN! ONE THAT I'M BREAKING TONIGHT!
UNH!
WUMP

I WANT NAMES, FAT MAN!
OF EVERY LOWLIFE THAT'S PAID YOU A VISIT IN THE LAST FEW HOURS.
ANYONE WHO TRIED TO SELL OFF A CREDIT CARD, DRIVER'S LICENSE, OR PIECE OF...

...JEWELRY.

BETTY'S PENDANT. HER MOTHER GAVE IT TO HER BEFORE SHE DIED. SEEN HER WEAR IT A HUNDRED TIMES.
STILL SMELLS LIKE THAT GOD-AWFUL PERFUME FLASH GOT HER FOR CHRISTMAS.
STRAWBERRIES.
IT SMELLS LIKE STRAWBERRIES.
LIKE BETTY.

WHO SOLD THIS TO YOU?!
HIS NAME! NOW!
HKK--
FINCH. HARLAN FINCH.

IT'D BE EASIER IF HE WORE A COSTUME.
A BIG, BRIGHT, STUPID PAIR OF TIGHTS.
WITH AN EVEN STUPIDER CODE NAME.
BUT ALL I HAVE IS HIS *REAL* NAME, SO THAT'LL HAVE TO DO.
WHERE'S HARLAN FINCH?!
I DON'T KNOW! HAVEN'T SEEN HIM IN--
MPHT!
HARLAN FINCH!
TELL ME!
AHHH!
I WORK OVER EVERY CROOK, THIEF, AND PUSHER I CAN GET MY HANDS ON!

WHAT ABOUT BOOMERANG?
OR THE OWL? I CAN GET YOU LEADS ON THEM--
I WANT *FINCH!*
TALK!
TOLD YOU EVERYTHING I--*UNH!*
--UNLESS I *WANT* 'EM TO!
THERE'S *ONE* MESSAGE FOR THE UNDERWORLD TONIGHT--
NONE OF YOU ARE SAFE UNTIL I FIND HIM! AND I'LL BE OUT HERE--AS LONG AS IT TAKES! I'LL BE RIGHT...

HERE!
I'M HERE!
HOW'S SHE DOING?! CAN I SEE HER?
FLASH! THEY'RE OPERATING ON HER NOW.
JONAH BROUGHT IN A REAL TOPNOTCH TEAM. THEY SAY THINGS ARE LOOKING UP--THAT SHE'S THROUGH THE WORST OF IT.

I SHOULD'VE BEEN HERE!
INSTEAD OF RUNNING OFF ON ANOTHER MISSION AS VENOM.
PLEASE. THERE'S NOTHING YOU COULD'VE DONE.

DID I HEAR RIGHT? DID SOMEONE SAY BETTY'S ON THE MEND?
THANK HEAVEN!
YES, AUNT MAY.
I NEVER SHOULD HAVE LEFT HER ALONE. NOT WITH--EVERYTHING THAT'S HAPPENED TO HER RECENTLY.*
FLASH, STOP IT. NONE OF THIS IS YOUR FAULT.
RIGHT. JUST WISH WE--I COULD GET A HOLD OF THE GUY WHO DID THIS TO HER!
*SEE VENOM #3 AND #4. --SYMBIOTIC STEVE.

WAIT A MINUTE... WHERE'S PETER?
I...UH... CHECKED IN WITH PETEY. HE WAS IN THE MIDDLE OF SOMETHING AT WORK AND--
MARY JANE WATSON! STOP IT!

YOU ARE ALWAYS MAKING EXCUSES FOR HIM!
WELL, NOT THIS TIME! THIS IS TOO MUCH!

MAN, YOU ARE IN A WORLD A' @#$%!
YOU GOTTA GET THE HELL OUTTA HERE! OUTTA THE CITY! THE STATE!
OUT OF THE U. S. OF FRICKIN' A!
WHAT'RE YOU ON ABOUT, SULLY?
LIVE NUDE
NUDE

ELLIE JUDE
TEL
IT'S THE SPIDER. HE'S AFTER YOU, FINCH! LIKE I NEVER SEEN 'IM AFTER ANYONE BEFORE!
YER DREAMIN'. THE WALL-CRAWLER THROWS DOWN WITH GUYS LIKE HOBGOBLIN...

WHY WOULD HE EVER WASTE HIS TIME...

...ON SOMEONE LIKE ME?
NEW SPIDER-TRACERS WITH BUILT-IN G.P.S., A COLOR-MATCHING L.C.D. COATING FOR CAMOUFLAGE...
...AND RIGGED FOR SOUND. I'M REALLY PROUD OF 'EM. NICE UPGRADES, RIGHT?
A REAL GOOD USE OF ALL MY PRECIOUS TIME.

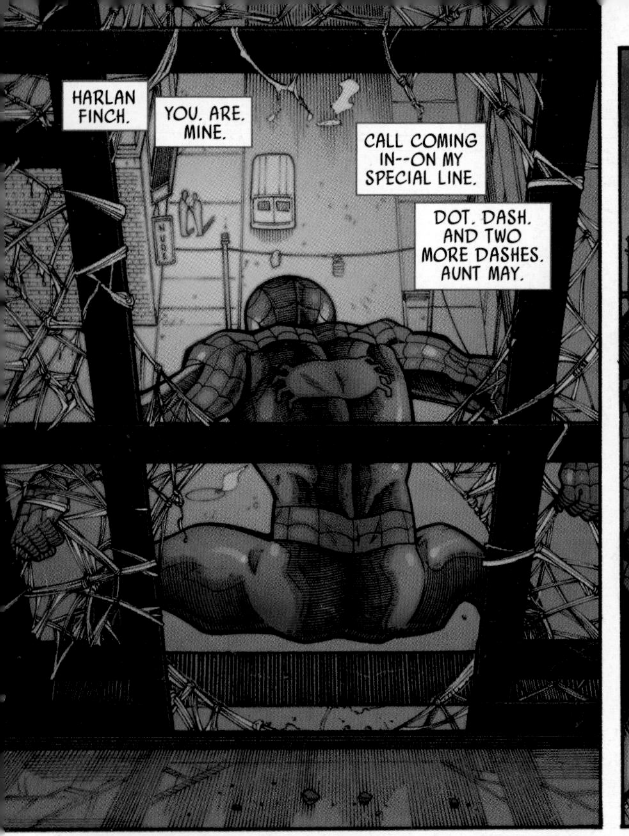
HARLAN FINCH.
YOU. ARE. MINE.
CALL COMING IN--ON MY SPECIAL LINE.
DOT. DASH. AND TWO MORE DASHES. AUNT MAY.
NUDE

ANSWER IT ON REFLEX.
AUNT MAY? I'M SORRY. NOW'S NOT A GOOD TIME. I AM AT--

WORK. I HEARD. AND I DON'T CARE.
DROP WHATEVER YOU'RE DOING AND GET TO THE HOSPITAL ***RIGHT NOW.***
YOU NEED TO BE HERE FOR BETTY.

NOTHING IS MORE IMPORTANT THAN THAT.
LOOK, I'M A LITTLE BUSY AT THE MOMENT. I'LL BE THERE IN A BIT.
ELLIE JUDE HOTEL
BUT WHY ***ME?*** WHAT'D I EVER DO TO HIM?
YOU WORRY ABOUT THAT ***LATER***--ONCE YOU'RE IN THE WIND!

NO! YOU HAVE ***RESPONSIBILITES.*** HERE. TO YOUR FRIENDS AND YOUR FAMILY.
AUNT MAY, PLEASE. YOU DON'T UNDERSTAND--
NO. I DON'T. PETER BENJAMIN PARKER, I SWEAR, I HAVEN'T BEEN THIS DISAPPOINTED IN YOU...
...SINCE THE NIGHT YOUR UNCLE BEN DIED.
WHAT?

DO YOU REMEMBER, PETER? WHAT YOU DID THAT NIGHT?
AFTER THEY TOLD YOU BEN HAD BEEN SHOT?

"YOU PITCHED A FIT...
WHO DID IT?!

YOUR AUNT IS NEXT DOOR. THE NEIGHBORS ARE LOOKING AFTER HER. WAIT--
I'VE GOT TO GO! I'VE GOT TO GET HIM!
"...AND RAN INTO THE HOUSE. BUT THEY WEREN'T GOING TO LEAVE YOU UNATTENDED.
"NOT A MINOR. AND NOT AFTER WHAT HAD HAPPENED.

"BUT WHEN THEY WENT LOOKING FOR YOU, YOU WERE GONE.
"THEY SEARCHED THE PREMISES. THERE WAS NO SIGN OF YOU. YOU MUST'VE GONE OUT THE BACK.
"MY HUSBAND HAD JUST DIED, AND THE BOY WHO WAS LIKE A SON TO ME, THE ONLY FAMILY I THOUGHT I HAD LEFT IN THE WORLD, WENT MISSING—FOR THE WHOLE NIGHT."

WHERE DID YOU GO?
AUNT MAY...I CAN'T...
TELL ME.

WHAT WAS MORE IMPORTANT...

"...THAN BEING THERE FOR ME?"

I'M SORRY.
IT'S ALL RIGHT. YOU...WERE A BOY THEN. YOU'RE A MAN NOW.
DON'T BE SORRY ABOUT THIS TOO. THERE'S STILL TIME.

I'M ON MY WAY.

OH... HI.
HEY, SLEEPING BEAUTY.
WHAT ARE YOU DOIN' HERE?

WE'RE ALL HERE, BETTY. JUST LUCKY YOU WOKE UP ON MY SHIFT.
THAT'S THE NICE PART OF THE PARKER LUCK.
REALLY? I THOUGHT YOU HAD THINGS TO--
PETER? YOUR EYE. WHAT HAPPENED?

BETTY BRANT. AFTER ALL YOU'VE BEEN THROUGH, YOU'RE WORRIED ABOUT THIS LITTLE THING.
LET'S JUST SAY I HAD AN ERRAND TO RUN...IN A PRETTY LOUSY SECTION OF TOWN.
BUT IT WAS WORTH IT. 'CAUSE I FOUND...

...THIS.
MOM'S LOCKET. PETER!

NEVER THOUGHT I'D SEE THAT AGAIN. DID I EVER TELL YOU? IT WAS A GIFT FROM MY MOTHER.
YEAH, YOU DID.
ON OUR FIRST MOVIE NIGHT.

CAN'T BELIEVE HE MADE IT.
OR THAT HE FINALLY TURNED OFF HIS SPIDER-SIDE... FOR ONE OF *US*.
YEAH. WELL, I STILL OWE HIM A POUNDING FOR TAKING AS LONG AS HE DID!
BUT I GUESS IT CAN WAIT.

IN FACT... WE BETTER GIVE 'EM SOME SPACE. THEY'RE GONNA BE IN THERE FOR AWHILE.
WHAT?! I'VE NEVER HEARD SUCH NONSENSE! I'M THE MAYOR! AND LIKE A *FATHER* TO THE GIRL!
WHAT IN BLAZES IS *MORE* IMPORTANT THAN THAT?!
IT'S FRIDAY.
IT'S THIS THING THEY DO...

"...IT'S MOVIE NIGHT."
HA. YOU'LL LOVE THIS.
A '50s MONSTER MOVIE? REALLY?
TELL ME IT'S NOT ONE OF THOSE CHEESY ONES THAT WRAPS UP WITH A BIG "*THE END*" AND A GIANT QUESTION MARK.
LIKE I'D DO THAT TO YOU?
The End...?

e Next Night.
CAN'T
ELIEVE YOU
YS FELL FOR
THAT.
LIKE SPIDER-MAN WAS ON A ONE-MAN HUNT TO CATCH--

...ME?
RUN!

AHHH!

NYPD
The End!

GOTTA SAY, AFTER FOUR STRAIGHT NIGHTS OF WORKING LATE IN THE LAB...
...IT'S NICE TO GET OUT.
BETWEEN, WHAT CAN ONLY BE CALLED, MY DREAM JOB AT HORIZON--DOING RESEARCH AND DEVELOPMENT ON JUST ABOUT ANYTHING I FREAKIN' FEEL LIKE--AND MY RESPONSIBILITIES WITH THE AVENGERS...
...THERE'S BEEN LITTLE TIME LEF TO HIT THE STREETS AND USE MY POWERS FOR GOOD, AS THEY SAY--TO HELP OUT REAL PEOPLE WHO MIGHT NEED THEIR FRIENDLY NEIGHBORHOOD SPIDER-MAN TO LEND A WEB
NOT THAT I'M COMPLAINING! FOR ONCE EVERYTHING SEEMS TO BE GOING RIGHT IN MY LIFE--BOTH AS PETER PARKER AND AS SPIDEY!
THANKS... BUT NO THANKS
written by Todd Dezago
art by Todd Nauck
color by Chris Sotomayor

YEAH, IF THEY WERE GONNA DO THE STORY OF MY LIFE RIGHT NOW...
...IT WOULD HAVE TO BE A BIG BROADWAY MUSICAL!
OH, THAT DOESN'T LOOK GOOD.
...NEED A LECTURE. JUST GIVE IT TO ME.
AND I'M TELLING YOU, YOU'RE MAKING A TERRIBLE MISTAKE. THIS MONEY WAS SUPPOSED TO GO FOR--
REALLY? REALLY?!
HUH?

IT'S THE 21ST CENTURY AND YOU'RE PULLING AN ATM HOLDUP? YOU DO KNOW THERE'RE CAMERAS, LIKE, EVERYWHERE THESE DAYS... RIGHT?
AND TO PULL SOMETHING LIKE THAT ON A DEFENSELESS OLD... ER WOMAN...WHAT'S WITH YOU?
OOF!
ACTUALLY... HE'S WITH ME.
COME ON, LEONARD.
UHHH...?
HE'S MY GRANDSON. AND THIS IS SUPPOSED TO BE HIS TRUST MONEY...BUT HE KEEPS NEEDING A NEW MODEM OR HARD DRIVE OR USB PORT OR WHAT HAVE YOU...
COME ALONG, LEONARD--THAT SPIDER-MAN IS JUST LIKE MAYOR JAMESON ALWAYS SAID HE WAS--A MENACE. READY TO PUNCH FIRST AND ASK QUESTIONS LATER...
AW, GRAMMA!
WELL...THAT DIDN'T GO WELL.
HAVE I SPENT SO MUCH TIME HANGING WITH THE 'VENGERS THAT I'VE LOST MY KNACK FOR THIS? AM I SO REMOVED FROM THE REGULAR PEOPLE--
THAT MAN--!
--THAT I CAN'T REACH THEM ANYMORE?
HEY! LOOK OUT!
HOOOOONK

THWAP!
SKREEEEEE--!
MST-300
--EEERT!
HU-- WHOA!
URK!
CAREFUL THERE, SIR. NEW YORK CABS AREN'T KNOWN FOR BEING VERY FORGIV--
WHA--! WHAT DO YOU THINK YOU'RE--?! I KNEW PERFECTLY WELL WHAT I WAS DOING! I DON'T NEED SOME SELF-RIGHTEOUS IDIOT DRESSED LIKE A GIANT INSECT TO "HELP" ME...! YOU COULD HAVE GIVEN ME WHIPLASH, YANKING A PERSON AROUND LIKE THAT!
DANGEROUS!
IRRESPONSIBLE!
AND THIS!! THIS...GOO! WHAT IS THIS STUFF?! I CAN TELL IT'S GOING TO LEAVE A STAIN. YOU'VE RUINED MY JACKET WITH YOUR...
AH, NEW YORKERS...NEVER ONES TO SKIMP ON THE GRATITUDE.
AND THAT IS SOME GOOD, OLD-FASHIONED NEW YORK SARCASM...

STILL, FOR ALL MY SUCCESS, THE GOOD THING ABOUT NEW YORKERS IS, THEY'LL NEVER LET IT GO TO MY HEAD...
ALTHOUGH IT WOULD BE NICE TO'VE HAD SOME POSITIVE INFLUENCE ON MY FELLOW MANHATTANITES TONIGHT.
MO' DOCTORS
MO' DOCTORS
THUMP!
HEY!

OKAY, HERE'S A SITUATION WHERE I CAN DEFINITELY BE OF SOME ASSISTANCE...!

HE TOOK THE ALLEY!
TURNER-- LET MATTHEWS KNOW HE'S HEADIN' HIS WAY!

AHH, NO!
YER KIDDIN' ME...!
YEEEAH... THAT WAS NOT THE REACTION I WAS EXPECTING...
NICE WORK, YA DOPE.
OKAY, SO... WHAT JUST HAPPENED...?
WE WERE LETTING HIM GO, YA IDIOT!
WE'VE BEEN WORKIN' THAT KID FOR SIX MONTHS, AND HE WAS JUST STUPID ENOUGH TO LEAD US RIGHT BACK TO HIS SUPPLIER...
'TIL YOU CAME AND...SPIDER-MANNED IT UP.
NICE GOIN', WEB-HEAD! JEEZ!
SORRY, GUYS--
I WAS JUST TRYING TO HELP. I MEAN, YOU CAN SEE HOW I--
YEAH. HEY, I GOT AN IDEA--
WHY DON'T YOU STICK TO THE SUPER-VILLAIN TYPES AND LET US TAKE CARE OF THE REAL BAD GUYS, A'RIGHT?

AND THAT JUST ABOUT DOES IT FOR ME.
I MEAN, TALK ABOUT YOUR NO-WIN EVENINGS. I GUESS FATE JUST FELT I NEEDED ONE MORE NIGHT OF THE OLD, OLD PARKER LUCK. NOTHING GOES RIGHT. EVERYONE'S A CRITIC.
DAILY BUGL
NO GRATITUDE. NO APPRECIATION.
SOME DAYS I'M NOT EVEN SURE WHY I DO THIS.

Meanwhile...
402
...THINK HE IS? ∻GRUMBLE GRUMBLE∻...ARROGANT FOOL...∻GRUMBLE∻... JAMESON WAS RIGHT!...A MENACE...
KARL?! OH MY GOD, KARL--ARE YOU ALL RIGHT?
WHERE WERE YOU? I WAS WORRIED SICK...
FINE, I'M FINE. STOP WORRYING ABOUT ME.
IT'S THAT DAMN NUISANCE SPIDER-MAN THEY SHOULD WORRY ABOUT. DAMN FOOL ALMOST KILLED ME.
WHO JERKS A 77-YEAR-OLD MAN OUT OF THE STREET WHILE HE'S CROSSING?
WHAT?! YOU WHAT?!
I WAS CROSSING THE STREET AND OUT OF NOWHERE THAT...FREAK...BUTTS IN, SPRAYS ME WITH THAT WEB-JUICE AND YANKS ME OFF MY FEET!
PRETENTIOUS PUNK! CAB. I SAW THAT CAB! I HAD PLENTY OF TIME TO--
CAB?! OH, MY GOD! KARL!
YOU WENT OUT AGAIN WITHOUT YOUR HEARING AID! I WAS WORRIED THE WHOLE TIME YOU WERE OUT!
THIS CITY IS DANGEROUS ENOUGH WITHOUT YOU NOT BEING ABLE TO HEAR ANYTHING, YOU STUBBORN OLD FOOL!
I TOLD YOU I WAS FINE. I DON'T NEED THOSE.
OH, YOU STUPID, STUPID OLD MAN. WHEN I SAW YOU FORGOT THEM, I PRAYED AND PRAYED FOR A GUARDIAN ANGEL TO WATCH OVER YOU, TO PROTECT YOU.
THANK YOU, SPIDER-MAN
"...OH, THANK YOU."
The End.

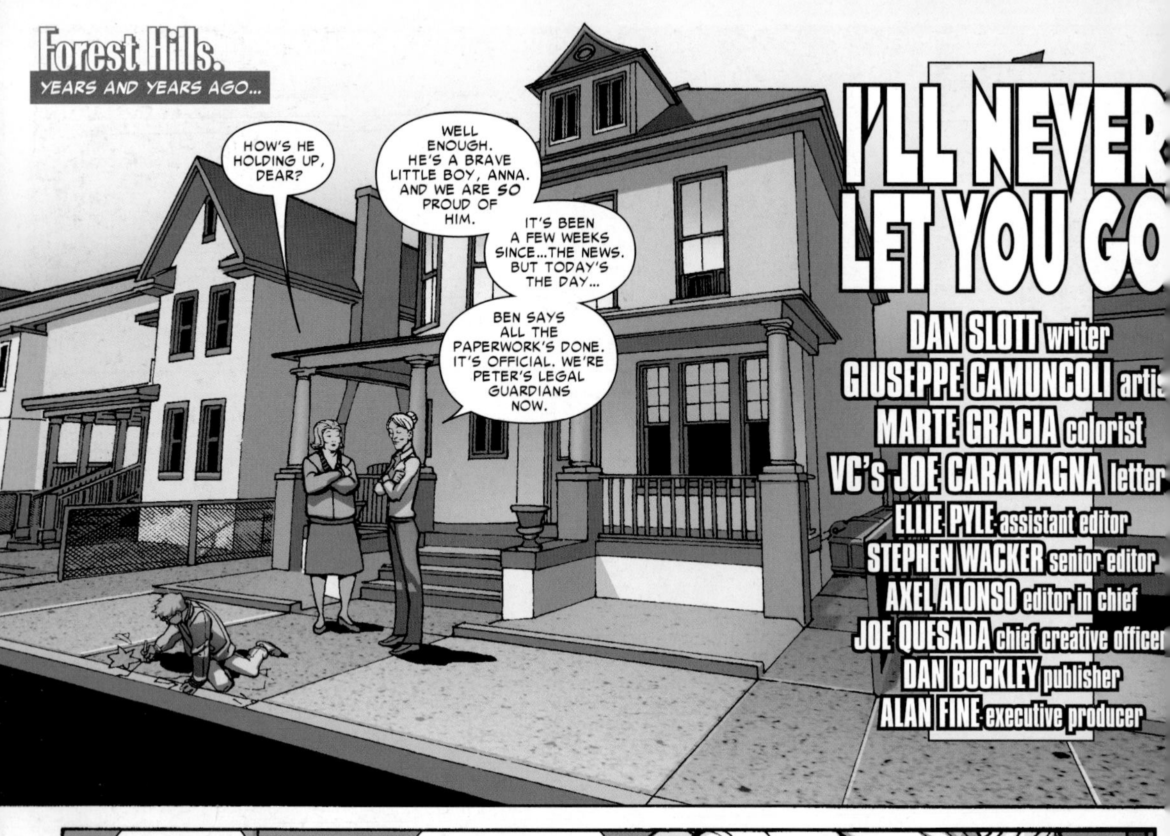
Forest Hills.
YEARS AND YEARS AGO...
HOW'S HE HOLDING UP, DEAR?
WELL ENOUGH. HE'S A BRAVE LITTLE BOY, ANNA. AND WE ARE SO PROUD OF HIM.
IT'S BEEN A FEW WEEKS SINCE...THE NEWS. BUT TODAY'S THE DAY...
BEN SAYS ALL THE PAPERWORK'S DONE. IT'S OFFICIAL. WE'RE PETER'S LEGAL GUARDIANS NOW.
I'LL NEVER LET YOU GO
DAN SLOTT writer
GIUSEPPE CAMUNCOLI arti
MARTE GRACIA colorist
VC's JOE CARAMAGNA letter
ELLIE PYLE assistant editor
STEPHEN WACKER senior editor
AXEL ALONSO editor in chief
JOE QUESADA chief creative office
DAN BUCKLEY publisher
ALAN FINE executive producer

I KNOW THIS SOUNDS HORRIBLE, BUT...
...THIS HAS BEEN A BLESSING FOR US. PETER'S WONDERFUL. AND BEN AND I, WE'D ALWAYS WANTED CHILDREN, BUT I-- I COULDN'T--
MAY PARKER? CONGRATULATIONS. IT'S A BOY.

MY GOD!
WHAT ARE YOU-- NO!

BEEEEEP
PETER!

GET OUT OF THE STREET!
SKRFF

WHAT WERE YOU *THINKING?!* YOU COULD'VE BEEN *KILLED!*
OW!
WHAPP!

YOU-- YOU'RE NOT MY MOTHER! YOU CAN'T--
I-I HATE YOU!

WELL, THAT'S FINE, PETER. YOU GO ON AND HATE ME.
IT WON'T CHANGE A THING. I AM ALWAYS GOING TO LOVE YOU.
ALWAYS.

YOU'RE LYING.
GROWN-UPS SAY ALWAYS, BUT THEY DON'T MEAN IT. THERE'S NO ALWAYS.
SOMETIMES PEOPLE GO AWAY AND THEY *NEVER* COME BACK.

NOT ME, BOY. I PROMISE YOU, NOW AND FOREVER. I'LL BE RIGHT *HERE*.
AND I'LL NEVER LET YOU GO.

Now. DINNER AT JAY AND MAY JAMESON'S APARTMENT UPTOWN.
PETER. CARLIE. JONAH. I'M AFRAID WE HAD AN ULTERIOR MOTIVE FOR INVITING YOU OVER TONIGHT.
WE HAVE A BIT OF AN ANNOUNCEMENT TO MAKE. WE'RE LEAVING NEW YORK.
REALLY? FOR HOW LONG THIS TIME?
FOR GOOD, PETER.
WAIT. THIS IS NEW YORK! WHERE ELSE IS THERE?! WHERE WOULD YOU GO?
BOSTON.
THIS.
THIS IS THE GREATEST INSULT IN THE HISTORY OF MAN.
DID YOU DO SOMETHING WRONG?
OH, THIS IS NOT GOING OVER WELL. PETER? SAY SOMETHING.
TRYING. THINK I THREW UP A LITTLE IN MY MOUTH.
WHY, JAY?
WHY WOULD YOU TWO DO THIS?
THIS HAS BEEN BUILDING FOR SOME TIME, PETE.
GIANT ROBOTS STOMPING THROUGH TOWN. ARMIES OF BUG-MEN OUT TO GET US.
MAY UNKNOWINGLY WORKING FOR THE HEAD OF A CRIMINAL EMPIRE!
AND WITH THE LOSS OF MARLA. AND WHAT JUST HAPPENED TO BETTY...
THIS PLACE ISN'T SAFE FOR OLD-TIMERS LIKE YOUR AUNT AND ME.

WELL I FOR ONE WON'T STAND FOR IT!
UM...
I'M THE MAYOR OF NEW YORK! WHAT DOES THAT SAY ABOUT ME?! ABOUT MY ADMINISTRATION?!
WHEN MY OWN FATHER THINKS IT'S TOO DANGEROUS TO LIVE HERE?!
SON...

DON'T YOU "SON" ME, YOU DRAFT-DODGING, HIPPY PEACENIK!
WHAT THE--?!

THIS IS YOU ALL OVER, ISN'T IT?! ANYTHING GETS HARD FOR YOU, YOU JUST RUN AWAY!
CARLIE, HONEY? YOU OKAY? YOU SAY SOMETHING?
NOTHING.

THAT'S HARDLY FAIR, JONAH. THIS ISN'T PERSONAL-- I MEAN, IT'S NOT ABOUT YOU--
AND IT NEVER HAS BEEN WITH YOU, HAS IT, "FATHER"?
WELL, GOOD RIDDANCE! NEVER SHOULD'VE LET YOU BACK IN MY LIFE IN THE FIRST PLACE!

JONAH! WAIT!
PETE, I HAVE TO GO, TOO.
WHAT? WHY? IF THIS IS--
NO, IT'S-- THERE'S SOMETHING I HAVE TO...CHECK OUT. WE'LL TALK LATER. ALL RIGHT?
OOOKAY.

SO...?
WHAT'S FOR DESSERT?
BOSTON CREAM PIE.
AND YOU WONDER WHERE I GET IT FROM?

AUNT MAY?!
PETER?! WHERE ARE YOU?
IN THE KITCHEN! GOTTA QUESTION!
COMING!
FOR SALE
Speedy Movers

WHAT IS IT?
SPATULA.
I CAN SEE THAT. WHAT ABOUT IT?
BEFORE I PACK IT UP...
ONE LAST BATCH OF WHEATCAKES? HUH? FOR THE ROAD?
WHY YOU LITTLE--
EASY, MAY. PASS THE UTENSIL, PARKER. I'LL MAKE YOUR WHEATCAKES...

...I KNOW JUST HOW YOU LIKE 'EM.
WHY, IF IT ISN'T THE WATSON SISTERS FROM NEXT DOOR.
OH, PETER! HERE. WE BROUGHT SOME SPARE BOXES.

ANNA, YOU'RE A GODSEND. FINALLY, I CAN GET SOME WORK DONE.
A CERTAIN SOMEONE IS TERRIBLE AT PACKING. HE KEEPS PAUSING AND GETS SENTIMENTAL OVER EVERY KEEPSAKE.
UNDERSTOOD, DEAR. LEAD THE WAY.

SO, MR. P, HOW YOU HOLDING UP? HAVING A HARD TIME CUTTING THOSE APRON STRINGS. ARE WE?
FAR FROM IT, MJ. COME WITH ME. I WANNA SHOW YOU SOMETHING.

LET ME GIVE YOU THE GUIDED TOUR OF HOW I SEE 20 INGRAM STREET. HERE'S THE PARLOR...
...WHERE I FOUND MAY SERVING TEA TO *DOCTOR OCTOPUS*.

AND THE STAIRWAY, WHERE MY DEAR, SWEET AUNT PULLED A GUN ON *THE VULTURE*...
...SO HE'D STOP MURDERING ME.
WELL, WE'VE ALL BEEN THERE.

IT GETS BETTER. THE BACKYARD HAS TWO OF MY FAVORITES.
THE WASH LINE WHERE *VENOM* HELPED AUNT MAY FOLD HER DELICATES.
OKAY, I GET IT. YOU MADE YOUR POINT.
NOT YET.

'CAUSE HERE, ON THIS EXACT SPOT, THAT PSYCHO NORMAN OSBORN, *THE GREEN GOBLIN*, TOLD ME HE KNEW WHO I WAS...
...WHERE I LIVED. AND THAT HE COULD COME FOR US ANY TIME HE WANTED.
HE...HE DOESN'T *STILL* REMEMBER, RIGHT?
NO. NONE OF 'EM DO. THAT--THING WITH DOCTOR STRANGE TOOK CARE OF IT. BUT *STILL*...

...I DON'T TRUST IT. I PLAY IT SAFE. AND I STILL WORRY. I'VE SPENT HALF MY LIFE WORRYING ABOUT AUNT MAY.
FAR MORE THAN SHE COULD EVER WORRY ABOUT ME.
HA. YOU DON'T BELIEVE THAT FOR A SECOND, DO YOU?
NO. AND, SURE, I KNOW SHE'LL BE SAFER ELSEWHERE. BUT I'D RATHER SHE WAS RIGHT HERE. ALL THE TIME. WHERE I COULD KEEP AN EYE ON HER.
SHE'S MY MOM, MJ.
PETER? CAN YOU COME UP HERE AND HELP US WITH THIS?
MOMMA TIGER'S CALLING YOU.
COMING!
Later.
I'M GOING TO START UP THE VAN.
PETE? YOU HAVE ALL OF YOUR OLD SCIENCE EQUIPMENT? BOOKS? EVERYTHING?
DOWN TO THE LAST DUST BUNNY.
SURE YOU DON'T WANT TO DRIVE WITH US UPTOWN TO JAY'S APARTMENT?
YOU GUYS ARE TAKING THE QUEENSBORO BRIDGE, I'LL BE ON THE WILLIAMSBURG. GUESS THIS'S WHERE WE SPLIT UP.
Speedy Movers
FOR SALE
WE'RE REALLY DOING THIS, AREN'T WE? LEAVING INGRAM STREET FOR GOOD THIS TIME?
IT'S OKAY, AUNT MAY. REALLY.
WAIT, BEFORE I FORGET...
...I GOT YOU A LITTLE SOMETHING.

HERE.
PETER! A RED SOX CAP? IN QUEENS?
YOU'RE GOING TO GET ME KILLED!

NAH, YOU'RE A TOUGH OLD BROAD. YOU CAN LOOK AFTER YOURSELF.
I KNOW.
AND THERE'S SOMETHING I JUST HATE SAYING TO YOU, PETER, BUT IT'S TRUE...

AFTER EVERYTHING I'VE SEEN OUT OF YOU LATELY, NOW MORE THAN EVER...
...YOU CAN LOOK AFTER YOURSELF TOO.
YOU REALLY CAN DO THIS WITHOUT ME, CAN'T YOU?

BUT AUNT MAY, I'LL NEVER BE WITHOUT YOU. YOU'RE WITH ME ALL THE TIME WITH EVERY CHOICE I MAKE.
THAT VOICE THAT TELLS ME WHAT'S THE RIGHT THING TO DO?
THAT'S YOU...

...YOU'RE ALWAYS WITH ME.
Speedy Movers
Speedy Movers
SALE

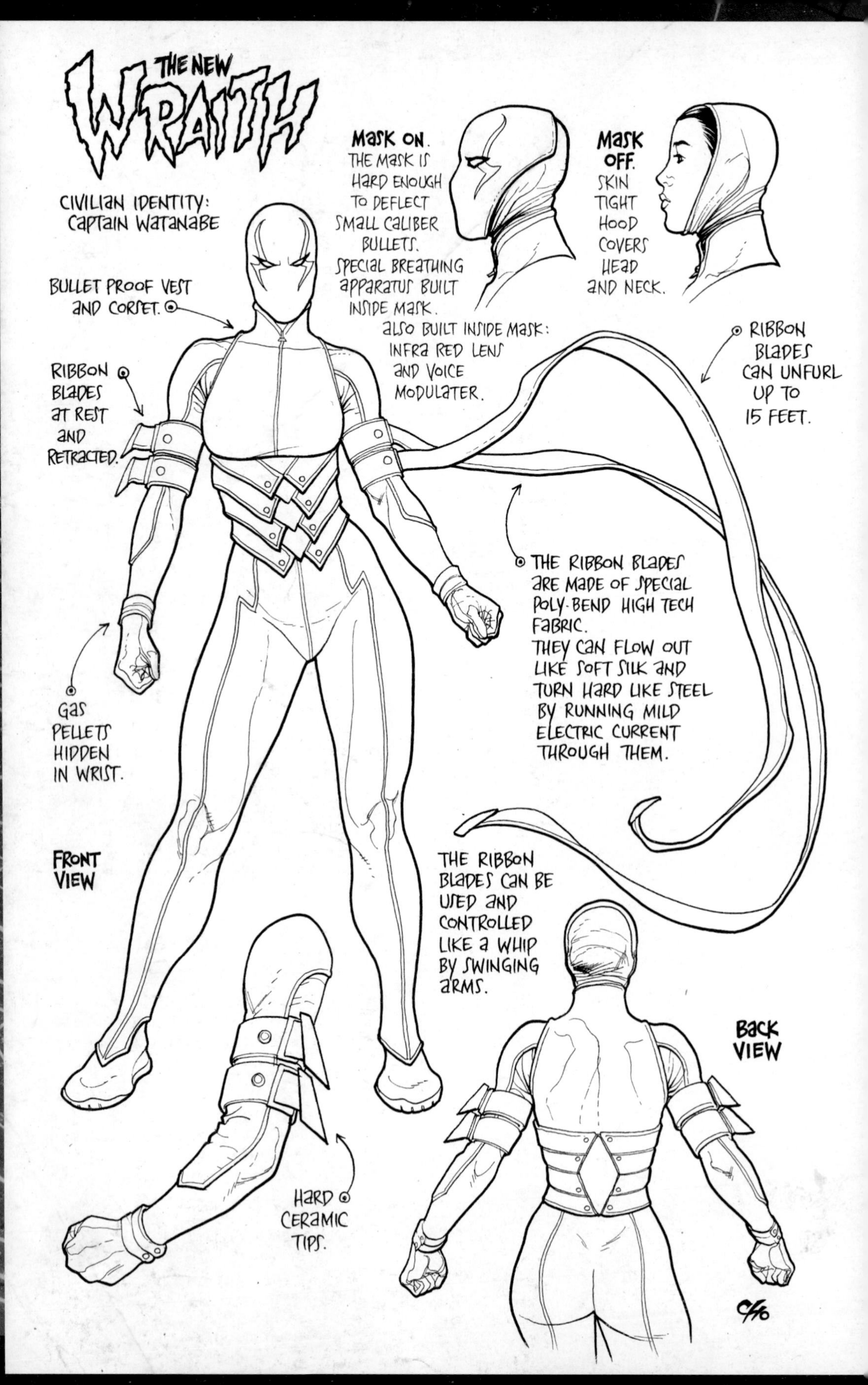

WRAITH DESIGNS
BY FRANK CHO